Securing the Borderless Network
Security for the Web 2.0 World

Tom Gillis

Cisco Press

800 East 96th Street

Indianapolis, IN 46240

Securing the Borderless Network
Security for the Web 2.0 World

Tom Gillis

Copyright© 2010 Cisco Systems, Inc.

Published by:
Cisco Press
800 East 96th Street
Indianapolis, IN 46240 USA

Printed in the United States of America

First Printing April 2010

Library of Congress Cataloging-in-Publication data is on file.

ISBN-13: 978-1-58705-886-8

ISBN-10: 1-58705-886-3

Warning and Disclaimer

Trademark Acknowledgments

Corporate and Government Sales

The publisher offers excellent discounts on this book when ordered in quantity for bulk purchases or special sales, which may include electronic versions and/or custom covers and content particular to your business, training goals, marketing focus, and branding interests.
For more information, please contact: U.S. **Corporate and Government Sales**
1-800-382-3419   corpsales@pearsontechgroup.com

For sales outside the United States, please contact: **International Sales**
international@pearsoned.com

Feedback Information

At Cisco Press, our goal is to create in-depth technical books of the highest quality and value. Each book is crafted with care and precision, undergoing rigorous development that involves the unique expertise of members from the professional technical community.

Readers' feedback is a natural continuation of this process. If you have any comments regarding how we could improve the quality of this book, or otherwise alter it to better suit your needs, you can contact us through email at feedback@ciscopress.com. Please make sure to include the book title and ISBN in your message.

We greatly appreciate your assistance.

Publisher: Paul Boger

Associate Publisher: Dave Dusthimer

Executive Editor: Brett Bartow

Managing Editor: Patrick Kanouse

Senior Project Editor: Tonya Simpson

Editorial Assistant: Vanessa Evans

Book Designer: Louisa Adair

Composition: Mark Shirar

Cisco Representative: Erik Ullanderson

Cisco Press Program Manager: Anand Sundaram

Technical Editors: Fred Kost and Patrick Peterson

Copy Editor: Apostrophe Editing Services

Development Editor: Deadline Driven Publishing

Indexer: Ken Johnson

Proofreader: Sheri Cain

CISCO.

Americas Headquarters
Cisco Systems, Inc.
San Jose, CA

Asia Pacific Headquarters
Cisco Systems (USA) Pte. Ltd.
Singapore

Europe Headquarters
Cisco Systems International BV
Amsterdam, The Netherlands

Cisco has more than 200 offices worldwide. Addresses, phone numbers, and fax numbers are listed on the Cisco Website at **www.cisco.com/go/offices.**

About the Author

Tom Gillis is the vice president and general manager for the high-growth Security Technology Business Unit (STBU) at Cisco, where he leads the company's businesses for security management, appliances, applications, and endpoint services.

Formerly vice president of product management for the Cisco STBU, Gillis was promoted to the VP/GM position after significantly growing its security business and market share. During this time, Gillis successfully led the Cisco product management team and outbound marketing, technical marketing engineering, technical publications, and training organizations.

Prior to his role at Cisco, Gillis was part of the founding team at IronPort Systems and served as senior vice president of marketing when the company was acquired by Cisco. Under his guidance, IronPort grew an average of 100 percent year-on-year for seven years. During his tenure, IronPort rose to become the leading provider of antispam, antivirus, and antimalware appliances for organizations ranging from small businesses to the Global 2000. Before joining IronPort, Gillis worked at iBEAM Broadcasting, Silicon Graphics, and Boston Consulting Group.

Gillis is a recognized leader in the dynamically charged and high-growth Internet security industry, with in-depth knowledge of the challenges surrounding secure network infrastructure. As an author, speaker, and industry executive, he has made invaluable contributions to the security technology community. He has presented at major conferences and events ranging from Gartner Symposiums to Fox News Live. Gillis is also the author of two books, *Get the Message* and *Upping the Anti*, a business guide to messaging security.

Gillis holds an M.B.A. degree from Harvard University, and graduated Magna Cum Laude with an M.S.E.E. degree from Northwestern University and a B.S.E.E. from Tufts University.

About the Technical Reviewers

Fred Kost is director of security solutions for Cisco and is responsible for delivering security solutions that enable Cisco's Secure Borderless Networks strategy. He has been involved in information security for 15 years and has extensive security experience with Recourse Technologies, Symantec, nCircle, and Blue Lane Technologies. Kost earned a B.S. degree in electrical engineering from Purdue University and an M.B.A. from the University of North Carolina.

Patrick Peterson joined IronPort Systems in 2000 and defined IronPort's email security appliances and also invented IronPort's SenderBase, the industry's first reputation service. In 2008, after the Cisco acquisition of IronPort, Peterson became a Cisco Fellow, a position that is reserved for individuals whose technical contribution has made a material impact not only within Cisco, but also in the industry as a whole. As a security technology evangelist, Peterson leads research projects to understand cutting-edge criminal attacks and business models and develop the technologies to combat them.

Peterson chairs the technical committee for the Messaging Anti-Abuse Working Group (MAAWG) and the authentication committee for the Authentication and Online Trust Alliance. He is a frequent speaker at industry conferences, including RSA, Gartner, Networkers, and AusCert. Prior to joining IronPort, Peterson served as vice president of engineering operations at Savi Technology, a leading provider of RFID solutions. Peterson holds B.S. and M.S. degrees in electrical engineering from Stanford University and holds patents related to antennas, radio frequency communications, and email authentication technologies.

Dedications

This book is dedicated to my wife Ally and my three children, who have tolerated late nights and weekend writing sessions to make this book a reality.

Acknowledgments

I would like to give special recognition to Kristin Potts, my colleague at Cisco, who helped project manage the book from start to finish, corralled sources, provided insightful feedback, and generally made this book happen. I would also like to thank my editorial consultants, Jane Irene Kelly, Christine Kent, and Nina Davis, who organized my ideas and turned them into the engaging text you'll soon be reading.

Thank you also to the customers, colleagues, and industry experts who contributed their time and ideas to this project—in particular, Richard Tedlow, Harvard Business School professor and business historian.

The team at Cisco Press, especially Brett Bartow and Dayna Isley, has been patient, helpful, and easy to work with—all the qualities that a time-starved author needs.

Contents at a Glance

Contents

Foreword

"I have been impressed with the urgency of doing. Knowing is not enough; we must apply. Being willing is not enough; we must do."

—Leonardo da Vinci

One fascinating aspect about technology and information security and assurance—if not the most fascinating aspect to me—is that problems and questions seemingly always come before solutions and answers, and the answers oftentimes prove quite elusive. It's like playing a game of chess where strategy, tactics, and time horizon connect, and you find yourself facing a skilled opponent who knows your weaknesses, and how to exploit them. This intellectual challenge of move/counter-move is energizing and exhausting, yet is never the same two days in a row. We face a seminal moment right now, today, in behavior and practice.

Within the past two decades as a practitioner in the Internet Age, I've observed four distinct eras that, in totality, represent the information security art form: Perimeter Security (Era I), Mobile Security (Era II), Application Security (Era III), and now Collaboration Security (Era IV). During the first three, exploitation speeds shortened, electronic crime became its own market, and layered technology became the defense—and also our weakness. And yet, the basic tenets for information security practitioners worldwide were the same—confidentiality, integrity, and availability.

It's time to add trust to the model.

This fourth era, Collaboration, is at least an order of magnitude more complicated to solve. The defense process is quite different and does not naturally build on past, and more traditional, practices. Information today is never simply "in" one physical or logical place. It is available for fast access, and its very location may not be well understood—it might be local, remote, in the data center, in the cloud, on the Web, on P2P, composed from multiple locations—and the list continues. It also may be on a PC; it may well be on a phone, a heads-up display, a television, or something that isn't invented yet.

We also became reliant on technology...somewhere in those 20 years.

Today, we are seeing signs that existing practices are fragile. Antivirus vendors are overwhelmed with malware, IP scanning doesn't work for broad IPv6 networks, and patching is nearly impossible because networks and infrastructures must support 7×24 operations. Our online world is viral, with more than 1.5 billion people around the world connecting, and the systems that support them are increasingly brittle, fragile, and vulnerable to disruption, corruption, and exploitation.

Plainly speaking, the information security art form, as we've practiced it for two decades, is inadequate for the threats we are facing today, especially when juxtaposed against how we are using the networks and technology in our daily lives. Perhaps that's why you are reading this book: Have you come to similar conclusions?

However, all is not lost. I find myself remembering a hobbit from *Lord of the Rings* saying, "Certainty of death, small chance of success...what are we waiting for?" Today and tomorrow's economies will base themselves upon cost-efficient, quality services where first-to-market globally defines the opportunity. It has also been stated that Web 2.0 and Security cannot co-exist and are, in fact, at odds.

I say, provided we have the courage to change course, and the conviction to believe, security as we know it will fundamentally change to face this new reality.

For our digitally connected world, the major influences for tomorrow's information security practices revolve around three important themes: technology evolution (in the forms of collaboration, virtualization, and automation), mobile user communities, and threat (both complexity and speed). Threat is at the list's end because it always seems that we focus on that first when, in fact, arguably it ought to be at least after we define what is valuable.

Mobile, connected, Web 2.0-enabled worlds are going to happen, and in some cases already have—whether we think we can allow them to or not. The human desire to communicate took a radical turn here, and it is fundamentally changing how we live, work, play, and learn. We need to adapt, as methods, not motives, are what need our full attention right now. This book seeks to do that and then provide ideas and answers to the problems it raises.

So turn the page...and as da Vinci observed, be more than willing, and "do."

John N. Stewart
Vice President, Chief Security Officer
Cisco Systems, Inc.

Introduction

In the 1880s, the advent of the railroad spurred the manufacturing economy. The railroad's capability to distribute raw materials and finished goods efficiently unlocked a century of economic growth.

In the 1980s, a similar revolution began with the introduction of the personal computer, the network, and the World Wide Web. These inventions unlocked the information economy, and we're still harnessing the full efficiencies and potential of this information economy. As with any economic development, up and down cycles, dotcom booms, and recessionary busts occur. But from a historical perspective, the opportunity for growth driven by continued refinement of the tools of the information economy has never looked brighter.

Imagine a business world in which information is efficiently available in the palm of your hand, with anywhere, anytime access. A good idea at 7 p.m. on a Saturday can be captured and efficiently shared with no friction. That world is here, and it involves some significant changes to the way we access and safeguard our valuable information.

Change creates winners and losers. The basic principle of Darwinism suggests that it is not the strongest species that survive, nor the most intelligent, but the one most adaptive to change. Change is flooding in to the corporation, driven by second- and third-generation web apps and handheld computing devices built first for consumers but irresistible to business users. Some companies have found ways to embrace these new techniques, whereas many others attempt to prevent their use.

For example, a national insurance company blocks its employees from using social networking websites and instant messaging—and finds that its policies are driving away younger employees who are hooked on Facebook and Twitter.

A U.K.-based marketing agency prevents its workers from using Google Docs, the popular online document-sharing application—and nearly started an uprising among employees who insisted they needed Google Docs to work with clients and finish projects on time.

Fearing data loss and security compromises, a healthcare provider in the Midwest wants to limit its practitioners to BlackBerry devices when they're working in the field—but their practitioners are pleading to use the Palm Pre or iPhone, which the provider doesn't support.

The wave of new collaboration and mobility technologies promise to change the way we do business and in the process create new efficiencies for businesses large and small. But with the new computing freedoms come new risks. The IT team is caught in the middle of two powerful countervailing forces: One is tearing down traditional enterprise borders, and the other is building those borders higher.

On one hand, new trends such as mobility and handheld computing are changing the way we think about enterprise computing. These always-on devices drive huge gains in productivity. At the same time, the rise of Internet-based collaboration techniques such as social networking, wikis, and high-definition video conferencing systems enable workers

xiv   Securing the Borderless Network

to share information more freely than ever before. Anyone who has joined a Cisco WebEx session from his iPhone can speak to this efficiency directly.

These new technologies are being pushed into the enterprise by enlightened managers who look to gain competitive advantage, or are being pulled in by workers who have used iPhones and Facebook at home and consider them basic tools required to get their jobs done. All these new trends are leading to more people accessing more data residing at more places on the Internet from more types of devices than ever before. This is driving a movement of openness in the enterprise, a trend we call the borderless network.

On the other hand, malware is getting more sophisticated, more malicious, and more difficult to detect than ever before. New technologies such as social networking sites, and a growing realization that employees need to mix some personal traffic with business traffic, are forcing companies to reevaluate their acceptable-use policies. And increasingly, companies are looking for ways to protect their sensitive data, either for regulatory compliance or to safeguard their most precious asset: information. These trends are driving the need for tighter security, or a move toward the closed enterprise.

And the IT team is often in the unenviable position of needing to restrict the business from operating efficiently, resisting new technologies and making users frustrated and angry—when the real value of IT is to become an enabler of new business efficiency.

When I visit with customers of Cisco and IronPort and ask them what their biggest security headaches are, they typically produce smartphones from their pocket, and say, "This." They're worried about workers accessing data on devices they feel they can't fully protect. And they know that this revolution is steamrolling ahead, whether they're ready for it or not.

The borderless network cannot be stopped because it is creating real competitive advantage for companies. At Cisco, the widespread use of its TelePresence high-definition conferencing system has cut the company's travel costs by more than $200 million and has increased the flow of critical information. Statistics like this cannot be ignored.

Although the tools of collaboration and information sharing are changing rapidly, so must the tools of security and policy enforcement change. These tools need to enable the IT team to embrace new technologies and at the same time increase safeguards over valuable information. IT departments must be enablers of new efficiencies and competitive advantage, not inhibitors. Wouldn't it be nice if the IT team could say, "Yes—use your iPhone," instead of always saying no? After all, everyone wants to be loved, even the poor IT team.

In the following chapters, we examine businesses that have embraced these new ways to collaborate and communicate, even as they acknowledge the security pitfalls. We explore the technologies that are revolutionizing business and the threats that have sprung up in the wake of these innovative solutions. And we learn how these threats are being corralled and managed, freeing workers to collaborate with confidence, no matter where or when—or with what technology—they choose to connect with each other.

How This Book Is Organized

This book begins by examining how Web 2.0 technologies are dramatically changing the way we work—and how we must think about network security. You learn about the challenges and threats today's businesses face as they struggle to fully embrace the value of mobility and Web 2.0 without sacrificing enterprise security. The book closes with a discussion about the intelligent, intuitive technology required to secure the emerging borderless enterprise.

- **Chapter 1, "Network Security—Yesterday, Today, and Tomorrow"**—Security was simpler when the security perimeter was a well-defined, defensible zone. But Web 2.0, mobility, and handheld devices have changed that. This chapter briefly examines the history of network security, including the evolution of firewalls, and asks the question, "Where do we go from here?"

- **Chapter 2, "Collaboration and Web 2.0 Technologies"**—This chapter discusses how collaboration and Web 2.0 are enhancing productivity and having a profound impact on organizations of all sizes; why easy online collaboration is transforming how people work together; the growth of enterprise-level online collaboration tools; and storage and applications in the cloud.

- **Chapter 3, "Building Relationships with Web 2.0"**—This chapter explores how one industry—financial services—is using Web 2.0 technology, such as social networking, to strengthen customer relationships, build new business, and streamline internal communications to create a more connected workforce.

- **Chapter 4, "The Cloud Computing Revolution"**—This chapter examines how two manufacturing companies use hosted, web-based CRM applications to streamline operations and create an environment for fast, seamless collaboration.

- **Chapter 5, "You're in San Jose, I'm in Bangalore—Let's Meet"**—This chapter examines the new generation of collaboration technologies, such as Cisco TelePresence and WebEx, that enable people to conduct virtual meetings from almost any point on the globe.

- **Chapter 6, "Watson, Can You Hear Us?"**—This chapter offers a brief history of communication and computing tools that have dramatically enhanced our connectivity and mobility—from Bell's telephone to the Osborne luggable to the Apple Newton to today's smartphones, including the BlackBerry and iPhone.

- **Chapter 7, "The Consumerization of IT"**—This chapter explores how there is growing demand in the enterprise both for, and for the acceptance of, new computing tools that first gain popularity in the consumer space. What impact is this trend having on security policies and the workforce?

- **Chapter 8, "The Bad Guys from Outside: Malware"**—Today's malware is smarter and harder than ever to detect. This chapter explains how malware creators ply their trade and examines the dangers that malware poses to enterprise security.

- **Chapter 9, "Who Are These Guys?"**—This chapter offers a deeper look into the world of online criminals and discusses how their business and economic models are constructed.

- **Chapter 10, "Signs of Hope"**—This chapter examines the signs that the "good guys" are succeeding in their battles to thwart online criminals. Security vendors use antimalware technologies and techniques that harness the power of the network and take advantage of processing power improvements.

- **Chapter 11, "Acceptable Use Policies"**—This chapter explains how the consumerization of IT and the growing popularity of handheld mobile devices are forcing companies to move away from antiquated notions of *how* employees should do their work. Meanwhile, management and IT leadership struggle to create realistic, enforceable acceptable use policies for the Web 2.0 world.

- **Chapter 12, "The Realities of Data Loss"**—This chapter explores this question: Given that the data loss problem is snowballing and compliance does not assure security, is data loss prevention even feasible? The answer: Yes and no. First, an organization must recognize that it cannot protect all its data. Second, it must realize that it doesn't need to.

- **Chapter 13, "Collaboration Without Confidence"**—This chapter pulls together discussions about security challenges highlighted in previous chapters and includes insight into how businesses are struggling to find ways to enable employees to harness the power of Web 2.0 tools and fully embrace mobile devices without compromising security.

- **Chapter 14, "Identity Management: We Need to Know if You Are a Dog"**—The ability to differentiate between individual users on a network and their levels of access and control is critical in today's computing environment. This chapter discusses how user identity is becoming a core element of enterprise security.

- **Chapter 15, "Security for the Borderless Network: Making Web 2.0 and 3.0 Safe for Business"**—Companies must accept that the Web 2.0 world is already here—and Web 3.0 is emerging. This concluding chapter discusses the secure borderless network and the need for intuitive security that is widely distributed throughout the network to enforce policies effectively. Also discussed is the Cisco vision to create an interface between policy and enforcement systems that is open and built on industry standards.

Chapter 1

Network Security—Yesterday, Today, and Tomorrow

This chapter includes the following topics:

- The Evolution of Firewalls
- Proxy Versus Stateful Inspection
- From Proxy to Stateful Inspection—and Back Again

The firewall is where our discussion about next-generation security for the Web 2.0 world—and beyond—begins. The modern firewall is the primary tool used by corporations to enforce security policies in the network. As we examine the security technologies that will enable us to secure the emerging "borderless network," it is useful to have an understanding of how firewalls have evolved.

When the Internet became widely available in the 1990s, information technology (IT) organizations were focused on ensuring and enhancing connectivity and performance—not network security. Everyone was racing to "get on the Net," and that mission overshadowed any thinking about, "Well, once we connect, how do we protect ourselves from outsiders?"

Of course, it didn't take long for hackers, delinquent insiders, and other malicious users to start taking advantage of weak, unprotected networks for personal gain, for notoriety, or sometimes, simply for the satisfaction of being disruptive.

As the Internet rapidly expanded and more businesses and individual users flocked to it for the purposes of work and play, network security quickly became a front-burner concern. It also spawned an industry that is constantly introducing increasingly sophisticated security technologies to the marketplace to protect the network and users from new and emerging threats, ranging from viruses and denial-of-service attacks to malware infections and social engineering exploits.

The first real security device designed to repel—or at least, impede—hostile intrusions was the firewall. The core mission of firewalls is to intercept and control traffic between networks with differing levels of trust. A firewall is part of the network perimeter defense of an organization and enforces a network security policy.[1] For most businesses, the operation of the firewall is still the major investment area for network security.

The Evolution of Firewalls

The network firewall appeared in the late 1980s in the form of a router used to separate a network into smaller local area networks (LANs). Security firewalls—routers with filtering rules—came into being in the early 1990s. They were effective but somewhat limited in their capabilities. In essence, just like a wall, they controlled access in and out of the network. And just like a wall, there were many ways for attackers to get around, over, under, and through them.

Fairly quickly, two primary approaches to building a firewall came into being: packet-level filtering and proxy-based firewalls. Of course, technology vendors did their best to differentiate their offerings in each space, but ultimately, there were two competing architectures.

"Initially, there were a variety of researchers working on innovative firewall technologies," says Joel Snyder, an internationally known expert in telecommunications, networks, and security. "But by 1995, everything had settled down into two approaches: proxy-based firewalls, a category that also includes application-layer gateways, and transparent stateful packet inspection firewalls."

In simple terms, a proxy-based firewall speaks the "language" of the application. In the case of web traffic, a proxy speaks HTTP and HTTPS. It terminates one connection and opens a new one, yielding a complete understanding of the data passing through. Here's a good analogy for a proxy: You call your friend John and his administrative assistant answers. You ask the assistant to ask John if he is free tonight to go to dinner. Thus, John's assistant is the proxy, terminating one conversation and relaying exactly the same information to the destination.

Meanwhile, a packet-filtering firewall is just a "bump on the wire" analyzing the billions of packets flying by and trying to piece together what they mean. Clearly, by operating at a much lower level in the network, the packet-filtering approach had the advantage of speed. However, the proxy had the advantage of intelligence.

Proxy Versus Stateful Inspection

The problem with packet filtering, Snyder explains, was that it was easy to fool. In response, the stateful packet filter, which monitors connections passing through the firewall and identifies a packet's "state" based on those connections, was introduced and positioned as a "smarter" packet filter. "The stateful packet filter was a huge step forward," says Snyder. "That's where the story of firewalls really opens. Everything before is not all that important."

However, what *is* important, according to Snyder, is that when the stateful packet filter was introduced, "it beat the crap, in terms of performance, out of every other firewall that was proxy-based." Again, proxy-based firewalls, because they operate at the more sophisticated application layer, were slow. So it was obvious almost immediately that the differentiator between stateful packet filtering and proxy firewalls was speed.

By the late 1990s, most firewalls had adopted some type of stateful packet inspection, and there was a great deal of improvement in areas such as performance optimization. However, there was a perception in the security community—due partly to the United States government's preference for proxy-based firewalls—that although proxy-based firewalls were slower, they were more secure. And that stateful packet inspection, although faster, was less secure.

"Meanwhile, those making stateful packet filters started saying, 'Well, you know, the security advantage that's claimed by the proxy people, we can simulate that,' using what has now become deep packet inspection," explains Snyder. "Essentially, the stateful packet inspecting people moved forward with their security, while the proxy people basically just stood still. One reason for their lack of action is that they were strapped for funds. Keep in mind that this was post-dotcom boom, and money for research and development was scarce. But frankly, no one was really pushing the proxy people to be more secure, either."

At this point, stateful packet filtering took an important turn. Companies developing this technology began adding features into their stateful packet inspection firewalls that made them arguably as secure as the few proxy products still available on the market. And stateful packet inspection technology kept progressing, with developers adding even more security features and focusing on delivering increasingly better performance.

Techniques such as protocol analysis allowed these packet-level devices to try to interpret the content of a data stream, something the proxy firewalls did well because they spoke the language of the application. However, even today, it must be recognized that a packet filtering firewall with the latest and greatest deep packet inspection has only a partial understanding of the traffic it is passing, whereas a web proxy can "read" web pages. Therefore, the web proxy has a complete understanding of the content it is passing. This is an important distinction that will become relevant as we examine the future of security in the emerging borderless enterprise.

Over time, the trend among firewall technology companies has become separating out each function into a separate "box" so that each can be done a little bit better. And more features can be added, which makes the process more manageable.

"This fits better into the organization of the company because the email people are separate from the security people," explains Snyder. "There has been an explosion of specific application-layer security appliances. Antispam/antivirus is one example. Content filtering, data loss protection, and intrusion prevention are others. There's a whole series of things that could've been done in the firewall. But rather than double-burden the firewall with this security technology, they've been broken out into separate, optimized appliances."

Firewalls have evolved over time and remain a core component of modern network security. They have become "specialists" that are *very* good at certain tasks, such as blocking unused network ports. However, to date, they have not been intuitive tools. They cannot determine the intentions of users or even, quite often, packets of data.

Most important, perhaps, firewalls cannot protect connections that do not go through them. Given the rise of remote working, the popularity of wireless, mobile handheld devices such as smartphones, and the use of online tools and technologies designed for collaboration, it becomes clear that the firewall simply cannot provide ample security for a borderless network. Walls, by nature, do not enhance openness or collaboration.

So, that's the firewall evolution—and where we are today. It began with proxy-based firewalls. Then, the stateful packet firewall duked it out with the proxy-based firewall. After the dotcom bubble burst, stateful packet inspecting firewalls became dominant. This made proxy-based devices less important in the security landscape—until now.

From Proxy to Stateful Inspection—and Back Again

In addition to performance issues, the big problem with proxy-based firewalls is that when a new application emerges with its own protocols, the firewall breaks the new application because it doesn't "speak" the protocol. For example, a new version of SAP with its own protocols would be incompatible with a proxy-based firewall that didn't speak the new protocol. This is a key reason why the industry has moved rapidly away from proxy-based firewalls to stateful packet inspection, which offers much of the security but doesn't break new applications.

However, the multiprotocol advantage of stateful packet inspecting firewalls is rapidly changing. Today, as nearly all applications move to a web interface, most firewalls have a simple rule that says, "Pass all web traffic (ports 80 and 443)." So, for most businesses, the Web has actually become a giant hole in the traditional firewall, where huge amounts of traffic flow through with little or no visibility.

Most major application traffic flows over the web protocol HTTP. In many ways, HTTP has become the new TCP/IP. It is the higher-level transport mechanism of choice for most applications. Thus, HTTP inspection capability is becoming increasingly critical to enforce security policies, and the need to have a proxy firewall speak multiple different protocols is rapidly fading. This has profound implications on modern firewall design.

Modern web proxies built for security speak HTTP at very high speeds and yield a platform that can enable more granular, intelligent controls for Web 2.0–oriented policies. A web proxy can readily tell the difference between traffic from Skype or Gmail or CNN.com or Salesforce.com, which allows for far more robust policy controls.

As these capabilities evolve, the web proxy begins to take on the functions of the core firewall—application-level access control. Thus, firewalls are making a multi-decade journey from proxies to stateful packet inspection and back to proxies, or at least, a hybrid of a proxy and a stateful packet inspecting firewall. It is important to note that the current IP, port, and protocol capabilities of a modern firewall will not go away anytime soon. But implementing basic policies at the IP, port, and protocol layer is becoming increasingly complex and insufficient in a mobile, Web 2.0 world. Thus, security tools—notably, firewalls—need to adapt to these changes.

However, before we explore what next-generation security should look like, we need to examine what's happening now in our Web 2.0 world—and how and why we got here. This can help make it clear why organizations embracing new technologies to stay competitive require a new breed of intelligent security solutions that can enforce more enlightened security policies that support collaboration and enhance productivity, while also protecting the enterprise and the mobile workforce.

Endnote

[1] "Firewalls and Internet Security, the Second Hundred (Internet) Years," by Frederic Avolio, Avolio Consulting, *The Internet Protocol Journal*, Volume 2, No. 2. http://www.cisco.com/web/about/ac123/ac147/ac174/ac200/about_cisco_ipj_archive_article09186a00800c85ae.html.

Reference

"Firewall Wars: Proxy vs. Packet Filter," by Joel Snyder, *Security Wire Perspectives*, April 1, 2004. http://searchsecurity.techtarget.com/news/article/0,289142,sid14_gci957738,00.html.

Collaboration and Web 2.0 Technologies

This chapter includes the following topics:

- Viral Uncertainty Principal

- Only Connect Digitally

- Easy Online Collaboration

- Enterprise-Level Online Collaboration Tools

- Storage and Applications in the Cloud

Not too long ago, Webvan was touted as the "third pipe into the home." Ouch—bad call. It's hard not to let the spectacular failure of the first generation of web-based applications create an overall cynicism about new technology. In the San Francisco Bay area, one can still spot a tan delivery truck driving around with the Webvan logo scratched out, like one of the ghosts of Web 1.0.

The hype cycle is an unfortunate but integral part of unconstrained capitalism. In retrospect, selling dog food online at negative margins was a bad idea. But it's probably a good guess that anyone reading this book was touched in some way by the irrational exuberance that accompanied the first wave of the Internet. So we're all a little guilty.

Irrational exuberance has a strong historical precedent. In the late 1880s, the onset of the railroad ignited the manufacturing economy. By 1894, after a frenzy of overbuilding, about 25 percent of the nation's railroads went bust, and investors lost huge sums. But the real winners were the companies that embraced the changes and created national brands—The Campbell's Soup Company, Heinz, Coca-Cola, and Ivory Soap, to name just a few.

We are still in the midst of a resurgence of value unlocked by tools built on the wreckage of the first Web. Web-based collaboration tools and Web 2.0 apps, along with social networking technologies, are having a profound impact on organizations of all sizes.

Web 2.0 has created huge opportunities for businesses to increase their productivity and efficiency. Whether they're using these tools to more effectively harness sales information, forge closer connections with suppliers, or distribute information in new ways, web-based technologies are creating competitive advantages for companies that can harness its power. Companies that embrace these technologies have the potential to break out from the pack the way the great consumer brands did in the late 1800s.

Even the most conservative companies have heard the clarion call. They're supporting BlackBerry use for key people, and they recognize that stopping productive employees from using their iPhones for work is doomed in the long term.

They also realize that restricting access to many of today's top websites and online tools—such as Google Docs, Facebook, or YouTube—can't last.

This chapter provides an overview of Web 2.0 and collaboration technologies that are rapidly gaining popularity in the enterprise.

Viral Uncertainty Principle

It can be hard for IT departments to know which Web 2.0 technologies to spend resources on. Those considered promising by IT staff or department heads might prove to have a limited adoption curve or shelf life. And demand for completely different Web 2.0 technologies might spread like wildfire within an organization, with employees wanting to use sites and tools they love at home at the office as well, and spreading them virally from there.

For example, a handful of years ago, setting up shared calendars and wikis seemed more likely to enhance an organization's productivity or sales than blogging or posting videos to the Internet. But abandoned wikis abound in organizations of all sizes, and while not all blogs remain vibrant, more and more nontech companies now have external or internal-facing blogs that are regularly updated.

Meanwhile, the success of online video as a communications medium cannot be disputed. With better Internet access both at home and at work, the interest in bite-size video that educates or entertains—or preferably both—is enormous.

Blendtec's "Will it Blend?" videos, which humorously showcase the capabilities of Blendtec blenders and are posted on the company's own site and on the video-sharing site YouTube, have proven to be one of the most effective viral marketing campaigns of recent years. Chevrolet asked website visitors to create their own mashup online commercials for the Chevy Tahoe.[1] Even Cisco, a techy company at its core, uses humorous online videos to market its products.[2]

Searching YouTube for information might outstrip Google or Wikipedia as an online reference tool. With more video content posted online every day—on YouTube, 10 hours of video is uploaded every minute[3]—the spike in volume increases the likely relevance of video search results, especially for information such as video news announcements or controversial or popular topical videos.[4] This trend means that online video with viral distribution is becoming a core component of how we do business and communicate with customers.

Only Connect Digitally

Then there are online social networks, which hit their stride in 2002 and 2003, when Friendster and LinkedIn were launched, respectively. The business-oriented social network LinkedIn lets users create online resumes complete with recommendations, connect to present and past colleagues, and ask each other for help finding talent and other resources. LinkedIn has become an effective tool for corporate recruiters in multiple markets.

The social networks Facebook and MySpace—originally aimed at teens and college students—are used for both work and personal life. Colleagues connect with each other on these sites, whereas companies are creating Facebook pages and groups for other Facebook users to join or posting news announcements on MySpace. Social networking enables people to make connections—personal or professional—that they couldn't otherwise make in the real world.

When organizations effectively use Web 2.0 tools and collaboration technologies, it can lead to measurable success not only in attracting users and building their loyalty, but building loyalty of staffers, too.

In the 2009 *Fast Company* 50, the magazine showcased one particular "startup enterprise" as particularly successful using digital and online tools; this enterprise took "a skinny kid with a funny name and turned him into the most powerful new national brand in a generation."

That startup: "Team Obama," which *Fast Company* named the World's Most Innovative Company for its broad-based embrace of digital culture and initiatives, using tools such as Facebook, MySpace, online videos, email campaigns, blog posts, text messages, and web-based call-banking to connect with supporters and likely voters. As the article said, "Barack Obama's presidential-campaign team relied on technology—what was known internally as the 'triple O,' or Obama's online operation—to connect with voters better, faster, and more cheaply than ever before."[5]

Other companies use microblogging tools—in which readers can read quick, short posts with a limit of 140 characters either on a webpage, or received them as text messages on their mobile devices—to connect employees to customers and each other.

Bank of America, Comcast, Southwest Airlines, Starbucks, and online shoe retailer Zappos.com all use the microblogging service Twitter to communicate with customers.[6] Although Twitter is a fairly public communication tool, microblogging services such as Yammer enable companies to create their own private network for internal communication.

Easy Online Collaboration

With remote teams a frequent part of today's work culture, coupled with faster bandwidth, better ways to collaborate online have become more important than ever. Google has been tapping into the home-office and small-to-medium enterprise market, buying online collaboration tool startups. The company also launched Google Apps, offering a complementary set of services that nicely integrate Gmail, shareable online calendars, and the Google Docs online collaboration tools.

Used together or separately, they make it easy for people to store and share documents online, share calendars and appointments, and collaborate on ad hoc or longer-term projects. All users need is an email address (which Google is happy to provide them), an Internet connection, and a web browser; they don't need to buy and install email or office productivity or online collaboration products.

Nor do users need to fret about where to store work, or how to manage version control; Google stores all its work online and lets users view past revisions and live edits as they happen.

Google Docs is so fast and easy to set up and use that employees in larger organizations are using it, too—sometimes to the horror of their IT departments. Why? Because IT doesn't have access control over it, making it insecure in terms of security and data loss. If employees have a login, there's no way for IT departments to ensure that they won't copy proprietary information stored in a Google Docs document or spreadsheet onto their home computer or a thumb drive for unauthorized use.

Regardless of the security concerns, Google Apps is playing a role in transforming the online collaboration landscape. Google was not first to market with several of the tools included in Google Apps; earlier shareable calendars and other online document collaboration tools exist. But Google's effective integration and generous storage policies, and the fact that the standard version of Google Apps is free to use, have made it extremely popular. Whether it will edge out mammoth office productivity app Microsoft Office any time soon remains to be seen, but in the area of ad hoc online collaboration for small teams and businesses, Google Apps looks promising.

Enterprise-Level Online Collaboration Tools

At the enterprise level, products for online collaboration range from Microsoft's SharePoint and Live Meeting to Adobe's Acrobat Connect to industry-specialty products such as Autodesk Buzzsaw and Cisco WebEx Connect, as well as eye-popping telepresence offerings from Cisco and other vendors. All of them are designed to make collaboration with remote teams easier and more natural and incorporate a range of access control, reliability, and security features.

At the high end, the new telepresence systems that have been rolled out in the past few years take videoconferencing to the next level. These latest telepresence systems incorporate combinations of top-of-the-line broadband, video, acoustics, display, projection, lighting, and room design elements that enable people from two or more locations to interact almost seamlessly.

Unlike earlier videoconferencing systems, there is no lag, latency, or crackly audio, and the impression of being in the same room with attendees is very convincing. The technology enables people to read body language, maintain eye contact, and make crucial meetings such as job interviews truly productive.

In today's environment, companies actively aim to reduce travel costs and time. So the role of enterprise-level collaboration tools and telepresence solutions can expand in enhancing the productivity of companies with remote customers or distributed workforces.

Storage and Applications in the Cloud

More and more organizations are using "cloud-based" applications and storage options—that is, solutions where the application and a customer's data reside on the Web. The benefits are efficiency, access, and cost. Companies don't need to make the kind of investment a major on-premise installation demands—or deal with the hassle, as most cloud-based systems aim to be as turnkey as possible. Companies also get anywhere-anytime access to data, and seats are easy to add or subtract as needed.

However, there are drawbacks. Some cloud-based applications, services, and market segments are far from mature. That means risks in areas such as vendor viability, potential regulatory concerns around data ownership and location, security and access controls, data segregation, and potential lack of insight into redundancy and data recovery.

Still, cloud computing and storage are becoming extremely popular concepts, and it's not just fly-by-night startups that are announcing products and offerings. Venerable companies such as Sun, IBM, EMC, and a host of others have entered the field, while many Software as a Service (SaaS) solutions are already in wide use. They range from solutions tailored to individuals and small businesses—Google Apps, SugarSync, DropBox, and Apple's MobileMe come to mind—to major enterprise players such as Salesforce.com and SAP. Then there are solutions that span both categories, such as Amazon's Simple Storage Solution and the many third-party front-end apps for it.

In the next three chapters, we briefly explore how different types of organizations use Web 2.0 tools and technologies—specifically, social media, cloud computing and SaaS, and WebEx and telepresence—to operate more efficiently and cost-effectively, enhance innovation, increase the productivity, creativity and cohesiveness of their workforces, and grow by strengthening relationships with their customers and business partners. These companies are good examples of the type of competitive advantage that embracing these new collaboration technologies can yield. Will they be the next Campbell's Soup Company? Read on.

Endnotes

[1] Farber, Dan. "Spinning the Chevy Tahoe ad campaign." ZDNet. April 6, 2006. http://blogs.zdnet.com/BTL/?p=2843.

[2] "A Special Valentine's Day Gift...from Cisco." YouTube Ciscovid channel. http://www.youtube.com/watch?v=3pffeMdDSoY.

[3] "YouTube Fact Sheet." http://www.youtube.com/t/fact_sheet.

[4] Helft, Miguel. "At First, Funny Videos. Now, a Reference Tool." The New York Times. January 17, 2009. http://www.nytimes.com/2009/01/18/business/media/18ping.html?_r=1&fta=y.

[5] McGirt, Ellen. "The Fast Company 50—The World's Most Innovative Companies: # 1." February 2009. http://www.fastcompany.com/fast50_09/profile/list/team-obama.

[6] Wortham, Jenna. "Problems with Your Checking Account? Try Twitter." The New York Times Bits blog. January 23, 2009. http://bits.blogs.nytimes.com/2009/01/23/problems-with-your-checking-account-try-twitter/.

Chapter 3

Building Relationships with Web 2.0

This chapter includes the following topics:

- Demolishing Communication Silos
- No Future for the Faceless

There's no question the financial services industry, tarnished by the recent economic crisis, has put a renewed focus on customer relationship management and image restoration. Some organizations are betting Web 2.0 communication tools are the key to regaining their customers' trust and earning new business. Many are also realizing how important these tools are for making a meaningful connection with current employees and boosting their morale and productivity. Others already sense Web 2.0 technology will likely play an important role in attracting and retaining financial talent in the near future.

According to a recent report released by market research firm Corporate Insight, "Social Media: Trends and Tactics in the Financial Services Industry," many major financial services organizations, including banks, brokerage firms, and credit card issuers, are experimenting with social media as a way to improve communication with their customers—particularly those in highly wired Generations X and Y—and to enable dynamic, real-time interaction among investors.[1] Among the tools being explored are blogs, podcasts, and online forums and communities.

This shift toward more personal, interactive communication tactics is significant for the financial services industry, which traditionally has been culturally conservative and generally standoffish with rank-and-file customers. But many well-known players in the industry have started reaching out to consumers more directly through popular social media networks, such as Facebook and Twitter, to strengthen their brand image and connect with and earn loyalty from customers.

For example, Charlotte, N.C.-based Bank of America Corp., one of the first major financial institutions to take the social networking plunge, has received positive media exposure about the valiant efforts of its Twitter rep, David Knapp, in helping to address an array of consumer concerns from questions about the reasons for overdraft fees to complaints about poor customer service experienced at a bank branch.

And since 2008, credit and debit card processor Visa Inc., headquartered in San Francisco, California, has been reaching out specifically to customers in the small business community with its Visa Business Network on Facebook. (Visa's pledge to give $100 in Facebook advertising to small businesses that join the community has no doubt been an effective way to build its following on the social networking site.[2]) As of September 2009, the Visa Business Network had started featuring blogs and Twitter feeds, and approximately 6000 members were actively engaging in the site each month. According to the network's Facebook page, more than 80,000 small businesses have joined the community.

To connect with its future customer base and potential employees, the Royal Bank of Canada (RBC) has been running the "Next Great Innovator Challenge" and related online community site since 2006. Teams of university and college students compete to develop the best suggestion for innovation for the financial services industry and can win financial prizes for their efforts. (In 2009, RBC asked competitors to "suggest innovative methods or tactics to transform the workplace to match the needs of an evolving and increasingly diverse workforce."[3]) Contest participants submit their ideas to the online community and can comment on or vote for others' ideas. RBC provides competition updates to the community by email, blog, RSS, and Twitter.

RBC's competition is not only an effective way to gather new business ideas, but also to engage a younger audience that is traditionally difficult for financial institutions to reach and inspire. San Francisco–based Wells Fargo also has been quite creative in its efforts to earn business from high school and college-age students. It created a free, online virtual world, the Wells Fargo "Stagecoach Island" community, where users can learn money management skills. Members of the community can create an "in-world" character and live in one of four "neighborhoods."(Think of the Electronic Arts computer game, The Sims.) Characters can build a dream home and work in a virtual job to earn "shells" to support the lifestyle of their choosing.

The financial industry is also paying attention to how individual investors of all ages are using social networks online. A 2008 study of U.S. consumers by Cogent Research, *Social Media's Impact on Personal Finance & Investing*, shows that social media influences individual investors' financial decision-making. The research firm reports that one in every four U.S. adults online engages in social media that deals specifically with personal finance and investing. It also found that investors are "highly engaged in social media, peer opinion influences a majority of investment decisions, and social media leads investors to question the accuracy of information delivered by official sources (advisors and investment firms)."[4]

According to Cogent Research, "online communities of like-minded investors are educating each other, and generating and sharing content on specific funds, products, and investment firms. This information is fast becoming a trusted resource for investors.... For example, more than half of high net-worth investors have questioned the accuracy of information received from 'official' sources due to social media, including more than a third of investors who question information from their advisors due to social media."

Demolishing Communication "Silos"

Web 2.0 is also changing the way some financial services firms and banks operate internally—particularly, how they communicate with and inspire their employees. Organizations are discovering that social media, when used in a controlled environment, is the trick to transcending demographics and engaging workers from Generation Y to members of the so-called Silent Generation (generally defined as those born during the Great Depression and before World War II). It also can help to make a geographically dispersed workforce feel more unified.

Wells Fargo is one financial institution fully supporting its employees' use of social media while on the job. It was actually the first U.S. bank to launch a corporate blog, in March 2006. Today, hundreds of Wells Fargo employees regularly engage in blogging— including video blogging—to share ideas with each other and interact with customers. The company's blogs have become so popular that they are the most-read nonbanking pages on Wells Fargo's website.[5] And ideas and comments submitted by workers via the company wiki are reviewed and discussed regularly by members of the bank's management team.

Another major financial institution in the United States recognized as far back as 2006 that social networking tools—including blogs and online videos—were the answer to boosting employee morale and keeping workers focused on productivity. One primary goal of embracing Web 2.0 technology was to streamline internal communications, so the bank's more than 1000 employees felt more connected to the organization—and each other—and would share news and ideas more easily and in a timely way. The bank did have an intranet, but engagement scores were woeful (less than 50 percent). Plenty of information was posted, but it was disorganized, staid and boring, and no one was paying much attention to it.

The bank developed an internal communications campaign, with social networking tools as the centerpiece, that would compel various groups in its workforce to step out of their comfortable communication "silos" and behave like a community. There was one group of economists who, for security reasons, primarily used its own intranet. There were bank examiners who were always traveling. A few hundred employees—many living out of the bank's home state—worked remotely. Rounding out the bank's workforce were several hundred operational staff who did not regularly access a computer while on the job.

The bank learned through its own research, including staff surveys, that employees were eager to feel more connected to the organization and their colleagues. They also wanted to receive more—and relevant—daily news and information in an engaging, entertaining, easy-to-absorb format.

In response, the bank's internal communications team completely overhauled the intranet and added blogs, videos, and other features designed specifically to engage employees. Email blasts are now sent out regularly to encourage bank personnel to make use of these tools, and many workers now participate in the bank's blogs. (Print communication efforts featuring intranet highlights have been distributed to employees with limited or no computer access so that they are not left out.)

Through the new and improved intranet, the bank's employees receive just as much information as before, but in a different and more meaningful way. And the positive feedback bank management has received from employees shows they not only enjoy the intranet's new format, but also actually look forward to visiting it daily, receiving and reading email blasts, and getting to know their colleagues nationwide better through social media.

No Future for the Faceless

These are social media success stories. But the banks' efforts to proactively embrace and experiment with new and innovative communication tools are extraordinary compared to the financial industry, as a whole, which is only just starting to dip its toe in the water—and most often, just in the interest of marketing. Although many banks expect to reap brand, cost, and customer satisfaction benefits as more consumers engage in Web 2.0-enabled methods of communication, the message to their employees about Web 2.0 and social media is often quite different, although very clear: No.

The 2009 Deloitte report, *Protecting what matters: The Sixth Annual Global Security Survey,* found that 36 percent of CISOs working in the financial services industry believe "the internal threat" represents the greatest risk to security for their enterprise.[6] This threat isn't just about the rogue fraudster who wants to find a clever way to rip off an employer, but everyday employees who inadvertently compromise security through their use of applications and devices not supported by the enterprise.

This is why many financial institutions do not approach their internal communications like the forward-thinking banks discussed in this chapter. Instead, they are either completely restricting or severely limiting the on-the-job use of social media by their employees for fear of losing valuable data, such as customers' personal information. They also worry about violating government regulations by not protecting that information, and possibly, facing significant brand, reputational and financial damage—and legal headaches.

However, despite the resistance many organizations have toward the use of Web 2.0 technology in the workplace, it's only a matter of time until they realize the restrictive policies imposed on employees must change. They will find they must engage fully in social media, internally and externally, if they want to stay competitive and attract and retain skilled talent—especially from Gen Y. They also need to seriously weigh the advantages collaborative Web 2.0 tools and technologies can provide to the organization, including cost savings and enhanced workforce productivity and innovation.

Very soon, there will be no place for the faceless financial institution of the 20th century. No one will tolerate having to press pound to talk to a customer service representative, or contacting an impersonal general inbox from which they receive no reply. The next generation of customers will expect to engage in meaningful dialogue with their financial services providers—in real time and with real people.

In fact, a 2010 Cisco Internet Business Solutions Group survey report about post-recession growth opportunities for banks predicts that, "to be successful with younger customers, a new approach to retail banking is required. Younger customers want banks to address their needs using the tools they and their peers have adopted, including mobile devices, video and social networking—and they are willing to switch to banks that embrace these technologies."[7]

In addition, the workforce of the (very near) future is not likely to devote their time and talent to an employer that resists change and wants to keep workers from reaching optimal levels of productivity and creativity. Thus, firms unable to reinvent themselves so they are relevant to customers and employees in the Web 2.0 world are likely to struggle—and risk fading away.

Endnotes

[1] "Corporate Insight Report: Social Media Redefining Retail Financial Services," *Wireless News,* November 1, 2008.

[2] "Visa Launches the Visa Business Network on Facebook; First of Its Kind Network Built on Facebook," Business Wire, June 24, 2008.

[3] "Next Great Innovator" competition blog, Royal Bank of Canada, September 23, 2009. http://blogs.rbc.com/innovator/.

[4] "Social Media Sharply Influences Investment Decisions According to New Study from Cogent Research," Business Wire, May 8, 2008.

[5] "Social Media and the Banking Industry," SocialMediaToday.com. http://www.socialmediatoday.com/ClientFiles/2b461d74-0b05-4149-a6fd-33257181a2c7/SMbanking_v1.pdf.

[6] "Protecting what matters, The Sixth Annual Global Security Survey," Deloitte. http://www.deloitte-ftp.fr/Publications/Mar_09/globalsecuritysurvey_2009.pdf.

[7] "The Next Growth Opportunity for Banks, How the Post-Crisis Financial Needs of Younger Consumers Will Transform Retail Banking Services," by Jörgen Ericsson, Philip Farah and James Macaulay, Cisco Internet Business Solutions Group, February 2010. http://www.cisco.com/web/about/ac79/docs/fs/nextgrowthopportunityforbanks.pdf.

References

"Bank of America on Twitter Solving Readers' Problems," by Ben Popken, January 23, 2009. http://consumerist.com/5137806/bank-of-america-on-twitter-solving-readers-problems.

BofA Help on Twitter. http://twitter.com/BofA_help.

"Creativity Where You'd Least Expect It," by Steve Crescenzo, *Journal of Employee Communication Management,* March/April 2008.

"Face-to-face king at the Fed," (Interview with Catherine Cummings), MyRaganTV.com, Ragan Communications. http://www.ragan.com/ME2/Sites/Default.asp?SiteID=2DE73B54303942C4AC9E7EC38 67DBF9E&Itemplay=58DAD73558564A1EB1D5CE7FC2BA5C63&tag=federal.

"Have You Visited Bank of America's Twitter Branch?," CreditMattersBlog.com, April 7, 2009. http://www.creditmattersblog.com/2009/04/have-you-visited-bank-of-americas.html.

"How the Chicago Federal Reserve raised its employee engagement by 52 percent," by Jane Irene Kelly, www.ragan.com, Ragan Communications, February 2009.

"Visa Jumps Into Social Media with Facebook Network," Small Business Trends, June 24, 2008.

Chapter 4

The Cloud Computing Revolution

This chapter includes the following topics:

- Managing the Islands

- Disconnected Workflows: Minimal Security

- Sleeping Easier About Security

If your business hasn't yet been touched by the cloud computing revolution, the day isn't far off. Nearly every technology industry watcher agrees that cloud computing is transforming the world of software. In fact, "the very confusion and contradiction that surrounds the term 'cloud computing' signifies its potential to change the status quo in the IT market," according to Gartner Research.[1]

What is cloud computing, exactly? At its simplest, cloud computing is "anything where you don't need to own your own physical infrastructure. Simply write your code and deploy it on someone else's servers," says Tien Tzuo, the CEO of Zuora, a company that manages subscriptions for Software as a Service (SaaS) providers.[2]

There are several ways to describe this trend, depending on exactly how you receive delivery of a particular software solution:

- **Cloud computing:** The concept of providing services over the Internet. Customers of cloud computing services "rent" these solutions and services from other providers, and thus don't have to host these solutions on their own computer servers or spend a lot of money buying the solutions outright. For example, when you use webmail services such as Gmail or Hotmail, you access a solution that lives "in the cloud."

- **SaaS:** Software solutions that are delivered using the cloud computing model.

- **Platform as a Service (PaaS):** Delivery of a computing platform—but not the applications—via the cloud computing model.

- **Infrastructure as a Service (IaaS):** Delivery of computing, storage, and network via the cloud computing model.

In this chapter, you discover why cloud computing is creating such a sea of change in the way that organizations share information and collaborate on projects. Figure 4-1 shows how spending on cloud computing is expected to grow through 2012. In addition, you learn how two companies saw dramatic changes in their capabilities to compete effectively and meet the demands of their customers using a solution that relies on the cloud computing model.

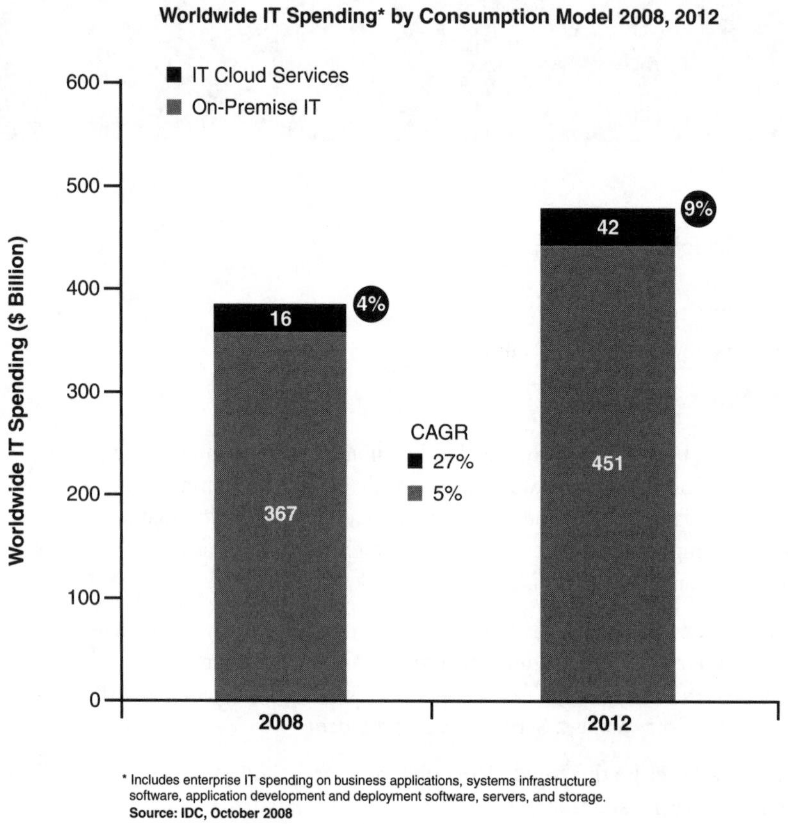
Worldwide IT Spending* by Consumption Model 2008, 2012
IT Cloud Services
On-Premise IT
Worldwide IT Spending ($ Billion)
600
500
400
300
200
100
0
16
4%
367
42
9%
451
CAGR
27%
5%
2008
2012
* Includes enterprise IT spending on business applications, systems infrastructure software, application development and deployment software, servers, and storage.
Source: IDC, October 2008

Figure 4-1 *IT Cloud Services Forecast—2008, 2012: A Key Driver of New Growth, http://blogs.idc.com/ie/?p=224, October 8, 2008*

Managing the "Islands"

Companies that juggle a high volume of complex information, often across borders and time zones, might reap the biggest benefits from the cloud computing revolution—for instance, meeting project deadlines faster, responding quickly to customer concerns, and developing products under tight timelines. These challenges can certainly be tackled without the use of cloud computing; companies can gain the advantages of speed, collaboration, and efficiency using traditional software installed on-site. However, cloud computing and SaaS applications can accelerate these benefits.

Manufacturing companies, with their complex web of sales orders, specs, testing reports, designs, and product documentation, flowing among far-flung shippers and suppliers, are perhaps most likely to benefit from SaaS solutions that enable this type of seamless, fast collaboration.

Two California-based manufacturing companies—Miyachi Unitek Corp. and Aerospace Composite Products—dramatically streamlined their businesses with Salesforce CRM, the cloud-computing solution for customer relationship management (CRM). Salesforce.com, the creator of Salesforce CRM, is by no means the only company making a mark in the cloud computing space; Oracle and SAP are key players, too, and many software companies now offer hosted or web-based versions of their products.

Companies that choose solutions such as Salesforce CRM to manage customer information and get a handle on the sales pipeline do so because they find cloud computing can provide a faster and more cost-effective way to compete. For instance, cloud computing solutions can speed time-to-market for products and can cut costs relating to collaborating in projects, such as delivery or telephone expenses.

Miyachi Unitek Corp. and Aerospace Composite are different manufacturing companies that came to the same conclusion about bringing more order and speed to sales management. Both organizations had a driving need to gather sales and customer information from an array of separate pipelines—such as sales reps and fulfillment—and place them into one bucket that's easy to access and always up-to-date. The easier and faster it is to find customer data, fill orders, and solve problems, the faster invoices get paid. And happy, well-cared-for customers are likely to keep coming back for more.

For Miyachi Unitek, based in Monrovia in Southern California, collaborating among employees, distributors, and manufacturing reps in 18 countries was an awkward process prior to cloud computing. The company manufactures equipment and systems for resistance welding, laser welding, and laser marking, all of which help bond separate materials into unbreakable units.

"We had an enterprise resource planning system—that was one 'island,'" explains Jim Malloy, vice president of sales for Miyachi Unitek. "Then we had a small CRM solution with no remote access, and that was very difficult to sync—that was another island. And then, we had a bunch of spreadsheets. Nothing was connected. We killed a lot of trees sending out copies of invoices and orders and quotes on a daily basis."

This shuffle of emails, phone calls, faxes, and paper mail took place among approximately 200 Miyachi Unitek employees, plus another 55 independent manufacturers' reps who sold the company's products around the world. This decentralized team also needed to stay in touch with—and manage—customers who were scattered to the four winds. "Our customers are moving manufacturing to lower-cost countries—from the United States to China, the United States to Central Europe, the United States to Costa Rica. You can't keep track of sales like this on spreadsheets," says Malloy.

Disconnected Workflows: Minimal Security

Aerospace Composite Products, a small, family-owned firm in Livermore, California, east of San Francisco, faced similar challenges to those experienced by Miyachi Unitek. The company produces composite panels, tubes, and rods for the medical and aerospace industries, among others. Although most of its products are created in Aerospace Composite's own factory, vendors and customers are worldwide. Justin Sparr, the company's vice president, was brought into the business in 2006 by his parents, who founded the firm in 1984 in their garage.

Although the business was successful, with ten employees and about US$600,000 in revenue, systems for managing customer information and orders were definitely stuck in the precloud computing age. "My dad did everything with pen and paper," Sparr recalls. "We didn't have a network in the office—just a series of workstations with different operating systems."

This disconnected workflow was a problem on several levels. "There was no collaboration possible," Sparr says. "For instance, when we did conference calls, we couldn't all see the same information like a drawing or an order at the same time. We didn't all have access to everything we were working on."

Sparr and other employees couldn't get an early start to the day by logging in to sales or project systems from home because there was no such data. With key suppliers and customers in China, or other regions several time zones away, Aerospace Composite employees in sales or production couldn't time-shift and solve problems before getting into the office. "It constrained the company to a nine-to-five workday," Sparr explains.

The lack of a system that could be accessed outside the office also slowed down the process of satisfying customer queries—or simply getting orders in the queue. "Say a client would fax in a signed purchase order," relates Sparr. "If George in sales isn't around that day, no one knows what that purchase order is connected to. The order would have to wait until George shows up. Same thing if a customer calls, asking, 'Where's my order?' If the person who took the order isn't in, nothing could move forward."

Sparr also spent sleepless nights worrying about the lack of security for critical company data, such as orders and design specs. "Working without any kind of centralized storage was a big liability," says Sparr. In 1996, thieves broke into the corporate offices and stole several computers, taking with them all the valuable records built up since the company opened its doors. Recalls Sparr, "We almost had to shut down the business."

So, the precloud computing scenario is now clear: Disconnected silos of information. Little to no flexibility for working offsite. Unproductive gaps of time where customers' questions aren't answered or sales opportunities aren't followed. No clear method for allowing nonemployees—such as sales reps or resellers—to get any visibility into sales and customer records.

Before cloud computing, the solution to these problems might have been a massive on-premise enterprise resource planning (ERP) solution. Price tags climbed to the hundreds thousands of dollars. And when a new version came out, you'd shell out more money. Systems were often extremely tough to integrate with other solutions. (And then you needed to hire pricey consultants to make everything "talk" to each other.) Their complexity might dictate weeks of on-site training for staff and—you guessed it—require that even more money be spent. See Figure 4-2 to see where cloud computing dollars are going in the near future.

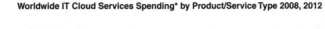

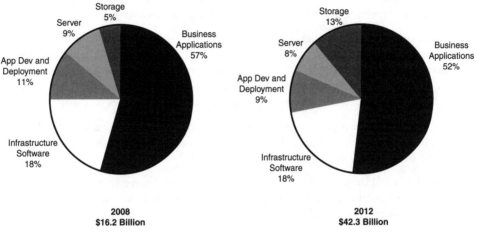

Figure 4-2   *IT Cloud Services Forecast—2008, 2012: A Key Driver of New Growth, http://blogs.idc.com/ie/?p=224, October 8, 2008*

The advent of cloud computing promised to make these problems go away, at least in part. Because cloud computing is web-based, deployment time is greatly reduced because no data center tasks occur, such as provisioning servers and deploying and testing the software. In addition, the clients are web browser-based, so no client deployment exists for users. Upgrades also take place automatically.

These solutions often replicate the look and feel of web solutions that people use every day, such as webmail or social networking websites, so they're usually no tougher to use than a travel website where you buy plane tickets. And you can log in anywhere you can find a web browser and an Internet connection. (These days, that's usually your phone or other mobile device, which means you can leave the office but still track down a customer order). Finally, because businesses usually pay for cloud solutions via license or seat fees, costs are spread out over time.

At Miyachi Unitek, the problems of dealing with manufacturing reps in several time zones and continents, and taking timely action on sales opportunities and existing projects, shrank dramatically. In a sense, the impact of shifting to the cloud-based Salesforce CRM application to manage sales and CRM was that the barriers of time and distance fell away.

Today, when Jim Malloy travels to China to meet manufacturing reps and visit customers' manufacturing facilities, he doesn't need to call back to the home office (assuming anyone is even awake) to find out what's happening with a new order, or if a new prospect has been contacted by someone in sales. He logs on to Salesforce CRM Mobile, the mobile version of the software, via his smartphone, and gets a view into every prospect or customer account: leads, quotes, invoices, orders, even lab reports on welded samples. Miyachi Unitek's two dozen sales managers and executive staff who use Salesforce CRM Mobile have the same ready access to sales and customer information.

"We're getting six more hours of productivity every week from every sales manager," Malloy says. "They're saving time because they don't have to make calls home for information, or wait until they get back to the office to update the sales records or update on the road late at night from a hotel. They can do this on their phones while they're traveling. That way, they can move sales opportunities forward in the sales pipeline."

The most salient measure of sales-oriented cloud computing is what it can do for the bottom line. Sparr credits Salesforce CRM for vaulting Aerospace Composite's annual revenue from $600,000 to $3 million in just a few years.

And at Miyachi Unitek, when sales execs realized they were somewhat short of their sales goals for the fiscal year, they could get a view into which deals were on the verge of closing and push them out the door.

At Aerospace Composite, a cloud computing solution has helped a small company act like a big company. "Information is power," says Justin Sparr. "Having it at your fingertips tells the client that you're in charge—that you have a command of your business. It's something I don't think my competitors have."

Sparr gets a leg up on the workday before he even gets to the office, logging in to Salesforce CRM from home to see which orders are being fulfilled and who's responding to which sales prospects. "It solved the problem of not knowing what everyone else is doing," Sparr says. "It also enables us to go after bigger opportunities that we couldn't have managed before." It takes fewer resources and less time to manage larger and more complex assignments when using an efficient cloud computing solution, he adds.

Jim Malloy's sales teams can also ratchet up customer satisfaction levels by tapping into a storehouse of product data. "If our reps are at a customer site, and the customer needs a manual, the rep can just pull it up in Salesforce CRM and email it right to the customer," says Malloy. "That was a big change of culture. They don't have to order documentation through the factory—and they don't have to worry what time it is in California."

Sleeping Easier About Security

Both Miyachi Unitek and Aerospace Composite rely on Salesforce.com's trusted infrastructure to keep their critical sales and customer data secure. If anything, knowing the data is off-site makes Justin Sparr sleep easier. It's not nearly as worrying as the possible theft of office computers, which could lead to the loss of every vital record (and password) in the company. "I never worry about that information," he says.

Malloy expresses similar confidence in cloud computing: "We've had total data integrity." He and other executives can set permissions and access for employees and reps at various levels, depending on what they need to see and when they need to see it."

Although cloud computing can typically offer excellent protection for data "at rest" on a server in the cloud, the disadvantage to the cloud approach is limited access controls. Most solutions offer username and password authentication schemes, but modern enterprises—particularly those wary about even doing business in the cloud—look for more security than simple authentication. A next-generation security architecture needs to address these concerns by placing advanced security in the network in a manner that provides consistent access control, logging, and reporting, regardless of whether an application is residing in a traditional corporate data center or out in the cloud.

Cloud computing stories, like those told here by Aerospace Composite and Miyachi Unitek, are becoming commonplace—and not only in the manufacturing industry. Cloud computing frees up people from working in silos, liberates them from the desktop computer, and lets them ignore borders and time zones. The impact of these efficiencies on any business cannot be overlooked. Still, despite these benefits, many organizations are slow to embrace cloud computing and other Web 2.0 technologies because of concerns over data security.

As should be the case when bringing any new technology into the enterprise, companies *should* talk security with their cloud computing provider, according to Gartner.[3] These questions should include the following. Where is the data stored? How will the provider handle potential security breaches? Who at your business controls access to different levels and layers of information? In other words, you need an airtight assurance that security is an integral part of any solution based on cloud computing. This is foundational.

Beyond these foundational security needs, the borderless enterprise needs tools that enable it to provide consistent, intelligent policy regardless of where the user or the data might reside. For the most part, these tools do not exist today.

Cloud computing is not just another buzzword or trend. It is a major shift in the IT industry that is akin to the development of power generation. During the industrial revolution, companies would make large investments in creating their own power generation infrastructure. Today, power comes from the grid (akin to the cloud) much more efficiently and reliably than home-grown power generation.

Cloud computing holds out a similar promise for modern companies. Getting critical enterprise apps from the cloud can reduce costs and increase efficiency for businesses large and small. The biggest stumbling block is security. Power is a commodity, but information is a differentiator. The technology industry needs to create tools that enable the enterprise to embrace cloud computing without compromising security.

If done right, the combination of cloud computing and advanced security should yield better controls than most companies have today. But significant work needs to be done to bridge the gap between where we are today and where we aspire to be. Fortunately, some major new technical breakthroughs, such as multicore based silicon, are making it possible to create the advanced security tools to enable us to embrace cloud computing and the onset of the borderless network, and to do so with confidence.

Endnotes

[1] "Gartner Says Cloud Computing Will Be As Influential As E-business," Gartner Research, June 26, 2008. http://www.gartner.com/it/page.jsp?id=707508.

[2] "Cloud Computing: How We Got Here," by Charles Cooper, CNET News, March 16, 2009. http://news.cnet.com/8301-10787_3-10196859-60.html.

[3] "Gartner: Seven Cloud-Computing Security Risks," CIO.com, July 3, 2008. http://www.cio.com/article/423713/Gartner_Seven_Cloud_Computing_Security_Risks.

References

Jim Malloy, vice president of sales for Miyachi Unitek, interview with researcher, March 2009.

Justin Sparr, vice president of Aerospace Composite, interview with researcher, February 2009.

Chapter 5

You're in San Jose, I'm in Bangalore—Let's Meet

This chapter includes the following topics:

- Breakthrough Technology

- Travel Costs Drop Dramatically

- Richer, More Productive Meetings

- Network Implications

In the weeks and months after the September 11 terrorist attacks, businesses around the globe came to the tough realization that they couldn't count on sending highly placed executives or technical staff to distant locations for key meetings. Disrupted airline schedules, security headaches, and cost-cutting in the wake of a mild recession all led companies to look at ways to connect, communicate, and collaborate without actually meeting face to face.

Webinars and videoconferencing filled the gap somewhat, but their technical limitations and inherently low bandwidth limited their application. Tinny audio and grainy video playback didn't exactly create a "just like you are there" experience, which meant virtual meetings were limited to a certain class of get-togethers, such as training sessions or sales support. In addition, setting up and starting meetings can cause headaches.

Enter a new generation of collaboration technologies that enable people to meet virtually from almost any point on the globe. It wasn't until recently that the components—audio, video, broadband, and a simple user experience—were put together in a way that made these kinds of virtual meetings equivalent to the experience of a live meeting.

For example, Cisco TelePresence offers a rich virtual meeting experience—equivalent to the experience of a live meeting. With single-screen or multiscreen conference rooms all over the globe, you can connect multiple locations on multiple continents in a virtual face-to-face meeting.

And WebEx, which combines online meetings with technology that enables people to share their desktops and view attendees using webcams, is another great example of this new generation of collaborative tools for communicating when you can't all be in the same conference room. Naturally, these collaborative and distributed technologies are all requiring a rethink of how enterprises manage security of information—you'll discover some of the solutions at the end of this chapter.

Breakthrough Technology

The technology that creates telepresence isn't brand new, but the effective packaging of the components is a recent development. For example, Cisco TelePresence, which launched in late 2006, brings together high-definition plasma TV screens, high-definition cameras, wide-band microphones and speakers, and consistent viewing experiences via similarly outfitted endpoints installed in rooms, offices, or cubes.

True telepresence aligns the various elements in a way that makes meeting participants forget about the technology. Part of the experience has little to do with the technology and everything to do with the lack of a complex user interface, and the room environment in which telepresence participants meet. If you're sitting at a desk in a room that looks just like the desk and the room that you see on the plasma screen, you're more likely to forget that the plasma screen is there. Cameras that fade into the background, and simple controls and scheduling contribute to getting meetings started in a snap. (In other words, you don't need to call in IT to launch a meeting.)

One of the reasons telepresence can re-create a live business meeting with such accuracy is that it is a well-controlled, reliable experience. If you're using Cisco TelePresence, you sit in a room with a half-circle desk, facing large plasma screens. You see the remote attendees at an identical desk, completing the illusion that you're all at the same table. With clear, high-quality audio and video, you quickly forget that you're talking to a TV screen.

Telepresence does what videoconferencing couldn't because it can communicate the subtle facial expressions and gestures that inform our communications with each other. Sure, videoconferencing enables you to see a colleague's face and hear her voice, but it doesn't let you "read" the body language and conversational nuances that reveal you're both understanding each other—and remind you that you are talking to a human. The fidelity of the telepresence experience is enhanced dramatically because of careful attention to detail. Each seat at the table is placed to focus on the screen on the other side of the conference. Microphones and cameras are perfectly placed to capture every detail. Telepresence includes carefully controlled lighting. Even the color of the walls enhances the experience to make the users forget the other person is virtual. The experience is immersive. Telepresence's lifelike experience preserves the nonverbal communications that before only in-person meetings could provide.

What is interesting about Cisco TelePresence is that the underlying technology—the audio bandwidth and video resolution—has approached the threshold of realism. Newer, higher-resolution machines will enable larger scale conferences and different formats. For the bread-and-butter business conference with 6 to 12 people around a single table, or hundreds in a large multipoint meeting, the cost of a telepresence experience will decrease steadily over time, driving ubiquity of the solution. In less than 10 years' time, it is not unreasonable to imagine that telepresence capability will be as prevalent as high-quality speaker phones in business conference rooms. Some companies are already taking a stance that all conference rooms should have telepresence capability.

Travel Costs Drop Dramatically

The technical advancements driving the adoption of technologies such Cisco TelePresence and WebEx are fascinating, but the real story is in what these technologies can do for your business. The numbers don't lie: At Cisco, use of telepresence to replace in-person meetings helped save more than $200 million in travel costs between late 2006, when its telepresence systems were deployed, and early 2009. And major manufacturer Grote Industries cut costs for its annual global sales meeting by 90 percent after it shifted to a WebEx-based meeting.

On top of that, there are tremendous savings in terms of employee time and productivity, because all that time spent waiting for delayed flights—or simply recovering from a 15-hour flight to Asia—is no longer a factor.

When Korea's Doosan Infracore bought Bobcat, the Fargo, North Dakota, equipment manufacturer, in 2007, workers were suddenly faced with collaborating with each other across an 18-hour time difference and 15 to 20 hours of flying time. Although executives were skeptical about getting return on investment from the cost of installing Cisco TelePresence points in Fargo and in Seoul, they saw the benefit of reducing the fatigue and lost productivity associated with the grueling travel between the two cities.

The company's heavy use of TelePresence meetings has already put a big dent in Bobcat's travel costs. "For that kind of trip, you do not have to avoid very many before the savings become large," reports a Bobcat executive.[1]

Cisco estimates that approximately 55,000 hours of lost work time have been recaptured, with an estimated value of $80 million (for the same time period—see Figure 5-1 for a comparison of videoconferencing and teleconferencing costs). The highest usage for the Cisco TelePresence system is between corporate headquarters in San Jose, California, and operations in Bangalore, India. (Usage is also high between New York and London, San Jose and Singapore, and the East and West coasts of the United States.) Given the 12-hour time difference, this means having to show up in San Jose in the evening for morning meetings in Bangalore, but it beats taking 20-hour flights back and forth to India.

When you talk about numbers such as $200 million in saved travel costs, concerns about the high cost of telepresence systems should evaporate. A Cisco TelePresence endpoint costs between $30,000 to $300,000 at each location; scheduling an hour-long TelePresence meeting, using suites at Cisco locations, runs approximately $300 to $900 an hour per suite, depending on how many people attend. No matter how you slice it, telepresence meetings cost less than in-person meetings over the long term. (They're also much more "green" than meetings that involve air travel and help reduce carbon emissions—a key benefit if your business is in the middle of an environmental initiative.) And of course, the core components are riding the consumer cost reduction curves, which means telepresence will become more valuable and more ubiquitous over time.

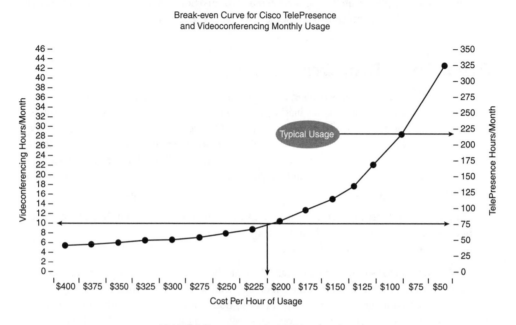

Break-even Curve for Cisco TelePresence
and Videoconferencing Monthly Usage

Higher TelePresence usage rates determine a low
per-hour cost compared to videoconferencing.

Figure 5-1 *Costs of Videoconferencing Versus Cisco TelePresence*

WebEx: Way Beyond Audio-Conferencing   On the website for Cisco WebEx, the conferencing and collaboration technology, is a cloud activity map (http://www.webex.com/activity-map.html) showing the online meetings facilitated by WebEx taking place all over the world. It's a fascinating display of how people rely on online conferencing to remain agile.

WebEx, which is owned by Cisco, is another piece of the "wherever, whenever" business story that telepresence figures into—that is, the story of companies that don't let a few thousand miles and a few time zones get in the way of success.

Just as telepresence collapses the time and distance barriers that can get in the way of collaboration, WebEx can create connections that previously didn't exist outside a conference room. Services such as WebEx have gone way beyond simply sharing phone calls. Today, CAD drawings, video, PowerPoint slides, and even training classes are exchanged, viewed, and edited in virtual meetings with co-workers, suppliers, prospects, customers, and students.

Another advantage of WebEx is that even the smallest company can operate across time zones and geographical boundaries. The use of collaboration technology enables small companies to compete against much larger firms, extending their reach and their products to any part of the world.

And like telepresence, the rich, multidirectional capabilities of WebEx can bring speed and connectivity to companies whose growth might have been stymied by the challenges of far-flung offices and punishing travel schedules.

As the worldwide economy began to wobble in 2007, Grote Industries, a global manufacturer of vehicle lighting and safety systems with headquarters in Madison, Indiana, began looking at ways to cost-effectively streamline business processes. For example, executives wanted to find an alternative to their method of distributing product information to salespeople via monthly mailings, followed up by quarterly on-site meetings.

"Under those circumstances, a product launch was very, very difficult to execute smoothly," says Chris Cammack, product marketing manager at Grote Industries. "Because everything depended on mailings and in-person meetings, it was impossible for us to help ensure that all salespeople had the same information at the same time."

By bringing in WebEx, teams at Grote no longer need to wait for product information by mail—nor do they need to coordinate their travel schedules to get to important meetings. Engineers can schedule meetings with vendors, and international teams can communicate in real time with clients and salespeople in Asia and Europe.

And WebEx gave new life to Grote's annual international sales meeting. "With the economy taking a turn for the worse, we thought that we would have to cancel the meeting," explains Dominic Grote, vice president of sales and marketing. "We wanted to avoid the costs associated with flying 120 people to a single location for a few days. But then we realized that we could make it happen virtually with WebEx."

Like some of the collaborative technologies discussed elsewhere in this book, WebEx relies on cloud computing for flexibility and ease of deployment. The Cisco WebEx Collaboration Cloud is a specially built network for delivering applications that enable effective sharing, and it also has significant security and redundancy protections built in to it. A multilayered security model protects on several levels: There's site security via customer-defined service administration; there's meeting security via permissions and user authentication; there's network security via SSL; and there's physical security for the WebEx data center.

Another key benefit of using a cloud-based conferencing solution is that it doesn't matter whether the other people attending your online meeting all have the same software. It's there in the cloud waiting for you to log in.

Architectural firm Kohn Pedersen Fox Associates (KPF) has studios in New York, London, Shanghai, and Hong Kong and needs to assemble teams of designers, engineers, and consultants for regular project meetings. It's a complex juggling act for the company, because collaborators are all over the world, and projects involve outside workers and employees.

For KPF, the answer was WebEx, which eliminated the challenges of looping in project teammates from outside the company and several time zones away.

continues

continued

"Travel is no longer a bottleneck in carrying out our projects. Execution moves more quickly and our teams optimize their time," says James Brogan, senior associate principal and director of firmwide information technology at KPF. "Our clients know that we can maintain more frequent contact with them, no matter the time or location. Especially in times of economic challenge, it's crucial for us to offer that level of availability while keeping our travel costs low."

Richer, More Productive Meetings

The benefits of using solutions such as telepresence don't just revolve around creating an in-person experience for meetings that you would typically—or ideally—conduct face to face. It's also about creating richer, more productive meetings across the board.

"[The telepresence experience] is so immersive that you can't multitask," says an executive from a global 100 high-tech manufacturer that uses Cisco TelePresence. "We accomplish more in three hours than in a one-day face-to-face. The atmosphere is much different and more focused in a TelePresence context."[2]

With telepresence, more stakeholders can come to key meetings and more voices can be heard—so more gets accomplished. "We're changing how we interact with our customers because of the video quality and simplicity of telepresence," says Rami Mazid, Cisco vice president, IT Global Client Services and Operations. "It's much easier for our customers to meet with our executives and technical experts when time and distance are no longer barriers." See Figure 5-2 for more on the drivers for telepresence adoption.

Telepresence can accelerate the process of bringing talent on board, which can give companies facing a shortage of skilled workers due to escalating baby boomer retirements a much-needed competitive advantage. It also means the field of candidates for hire can be widened far beyond the local—or even national—employment market.

Cisco executives already use Cisco TelePresence to interview job candidates faster, and even hire them, without meeting them in the flesh. Before telepresence, they never would have been confident enough to make key hires in the absence of an in-person interview.

"I can conduct performance reviews and other meetings that I never would have done over a conference call or even a video conference," says Joe Duarte, a Cisco senior systems engineering manager. "You can see a person's reactions, which gives me comfort as a manager to have remote meetings in this way."

For companies doing business on the global stage, telepresence can speed up the pace at which you operate. For example, top executives can be more agile when they don't have to worry about booking a 15-hour flight to China to consider a potential acquisition. Or if a corporate crisis hits, management can call a critical meeting with corporate heads around the globe, without worrying that they won't make it into the boardroom before the front-page story from The New York Times hits the Web.

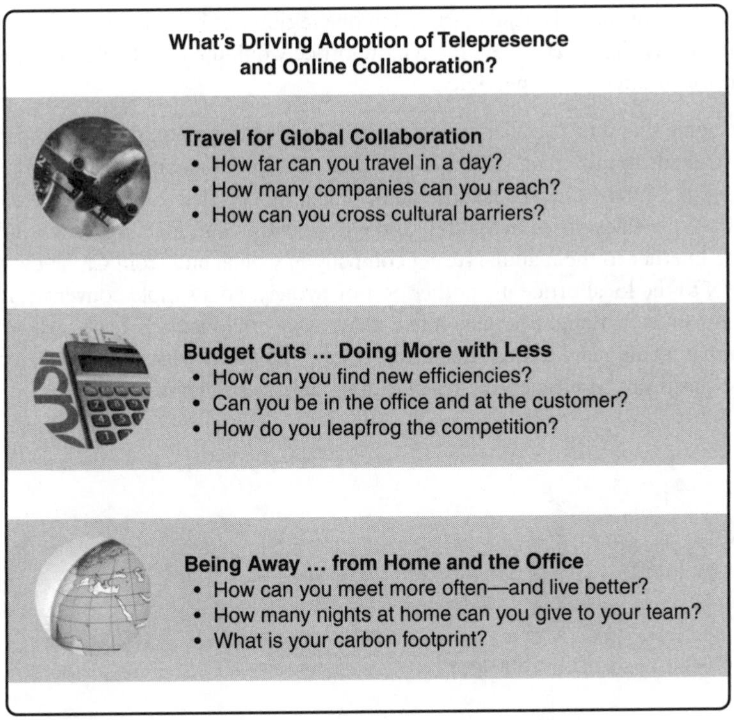

Figure 5-2 *What's Driving Adoption of Telepresence and Online Collaboration*

And any executive who has ever had to miss his or her child's soccer games because of business travel can relate to the quality-of-life benefits telepresence brings. You can meet in the morning with London, check in with the New York office over lunch, talk to Tokyo in the afternoon, and get home in time for dinner.

Network Implications

The development of telepresence, and more broadly the use of video for business communications, is likely to have a profound impact on the way that companies architect their networks. Traditionally, the global business would set up a hub-and-spoke model, in which each location of a business would "backhaul" traffic to a small number of Internet access points around the world. With this system, security devices such as firewalls and proxies can be fairly easily inserted at the "head end" or hub, and corporate policy can be enforced.

However, as we contemplate a world in which employees in all aspects of the business are communicating with other people in other businesses, the sheer volume and performance requirements of the traffic profile forces a rethinking of the network architecture.

Currently, if a business is headquartered in one region but has a remote office in another, it is most likely that traffic from the remote office would be backhauled to headquarters for controlled Internet connectivity.

Let's imagine that an Australian salesperson at a networking equipment company based in San Jose needs to talk to an Australia-based IT manager at an auto manufacturer head-quartered in China. With the traditional backhaul model, the video stream would need to travel from the sales office in Sydney to the head end in San Jose. There it will be routed over the Internet to the manufacturing company in China, and from China over a site-to-site VPN to the local office in another part of Sydney. So a simple conversation between two companies that might be only a few miles away could launch a large 10-MB data stream that would need to be transmitted around the globe with near-zero latency. Clearly, this is not an efficient or scalable approach, as shown in Figure 5-3.

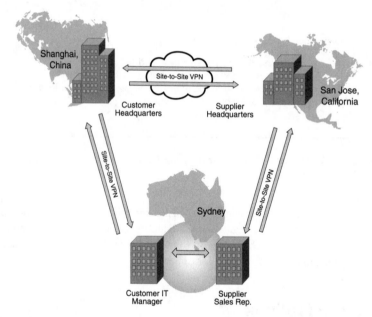

Figure 5-3 *The Disadvantages of Backhauled Internet Traffic*

The use of business video, and particularly the high-resolution streams of telepresence, is leading to the increased use of local Internet access—or what many analysts refer to as the dissolving corporate perimeter or the borderless network. This new traffic type, more than any other trend, is driving customers to consider local Internet access. And if one is going to poke a hole in the traditional perimeter for video, why not use local access for all traffic types?

The answer is security. If a business with 30 remote sites around the world enables each site to directly access the Internet, it needs to somehow deploy security at each of the 30 "holes" it pokes in that traditional corporate perimeter. For traditional "box-based" security, this would mean deploying and managing 30 (or maybe even 90) boxes in 30 locations around the world—not a small task.

In the next five years, as mobility, business video, and Software-as-a-Service applications take hold, the traditional notion of a hard perimeter will be gone, and enterprises will move to a borderless network model. In a borderless enterprise, we need to consider ways to put security enforcement into the "capillaries" of the network, or into the cloud itself. This needs to be done without dropping separate boxes into every location. This way, a business can enforce its security policy no matter where its users are—at a branch office, at a coffee shop, or at an airport.

The traditional corporate perimeter is dissolving—that's a recognized trend. What's not as clear is what the tools will look like to provide consistent security policy on this distributed, mobile workforce. We explore the vision for this distributed enterprise security in subsequent chapters.

Endnotes

[1] Forbes, Harry. *Cisco TelePresence in Manufacturing: Changing Behavior for Enhanced Collaboration*, February 23, 2009, ARC Advisory Group. www.ARCweb.com.

[2] Ibid.

References

ARC Advisory Group, "Cisco TelePresence in Manufacturing: Changing Behavior for Enhanced Collaboration," February 23, 2009.
http://www.cisco.com/en/US/prod/collateral/ps7060/ps8329/ps8330/ps9599/ARC_TelePresence_WP_02_23_09_Final.pdf.

Cisco Systems, "How Virtual Meetings Provide Substantial Business Value and User Benefits."
http://www.cisco.com/web/about/ciscoitatwork/downloads/ciscoitatwork/pdf/Cisco_IT_Case_Study_TelePresence_Benefits.pdf.

Cisco WebEx case study, "Kohn Pedersen Fox expedites global projects with WebEx."
http://webex.com/fileadmin/webex/documents/enterprise/pdf/Other/casestudy_kpf.pdf.

Cisco WebEx case study, "Manufacturer Outpaces Competition with Virtual Meetings."
http://webex.com/fileadmin/webex09/files_en_us/pdf/casestudies/Grote_CS_D2.pdf.

Chapter 6

Watson, Can You Hear Us?

This chapter includes the following topics:

- Human Need for Connectedness

- Cutting the Cord

- One Chip Makes You Smaller

- Handheld Harvest: Apples to BlackBerrys

- These Unprecedented Times

- Evolution of the Smartphone

Unquestionably, organizations and individuals are achieving far greater levels of productivity and efficiency—and often, significant cost savings—than ever before through the use of Web 2.0 technology. But increasingly sophisticated communication and business tools such as online meeting applications, telepresence, social media, cloud computing, and Software-as-a-Service (SaaS) are only part of what's driving this trend: Mobile devices, such as smartphones, are placing the power of Web 2.0 right in the palms of our hands.

Although we might marvel at how quickly handheld computing has advanced in recent years, this evolution is just one more step forward—albeit a big step—on the long, historical path of information processing and sharing in our society, according to Harvard Business School professor and business historian, Richard S. Tedlow.

"Today's smartphone is a combination of all the major technological revolutions [since the 19th century]—from the telegraph to the telephone to the PC to the Internet," says Tedlow, who is also the first resident scholar at The Computer History Museum in Mountain View, California. "But this isn't just a case of the spork—a spoon and a fork that, when combined, are less useful than when separate. The converged communications of the smartphone will be the foundation for decades of efficiency improvements and, therefore, productivity growth."

To fully understand the impact the smartphone and the evolved computing model are poised to make on our future, it is useful to consider a historical perspective on communication and computing technology, so we can understand what brought us to this critical point of convergence.

Human Need for Connectedness

People had been dotting and dashing Morse code messages with the telegraph for decades before inventor Alexander Graham Bell—who had been conducting experiments to find ways to improve telegraph communications so multiple messages could be transmitted over the same wire—made what is widely considered to be the first (intelligible) electronic speech transmission. In his Boston laboratory, he reportedly said to his assistant, Thomas A. Watson, via a device called a liquid transmitter, "Mr. Watson, come here, I want you."[1]

By 1877, the Bell Telephone Company had been founded and the first commercial telephone—a single transmitter/receiver contained in a rectangular wooden box—was in use and quickly gaining fame worldwide (see Figure 6-1). Whereas the telegraph had been used primarily by railways and for relaying stock prices and market news to interested parties, the telephone, because it enabled person-to-person *conversation*, represented the potential for anyone to engage in information exchange that was far more immediate, intimate, and personalized.

Figure 6-1 *Unassuming: Bell's First Commercial Telephone*

The first private phone lines were generally between a wealthy or privileged person's home and his place of business, but telephone exchanges for "subscribers" soon followed. In the 1890s, telephone use experienced a boom not unlike Internet adoption in the 1990s, but it would still take decades for the technology to truly become commonplace.

However, even in those early days of the telephone's existence, Bell clearly understood the role it would play in connecting the world and enabling people to "reach out and touch someone." In 1878, he wrote, "'I believe in the future wires will unite the head offices of telephone companies in different cities, and a man in one part of the country may communicate by word of mouth with another in a distant place.'"[2]

Cutting the Cord

Over the next century, Bell's prediction certainly came to fruition—and then some. Just as our modern society is determined to make reliable Internet access and cell phone coverage available everywhere, a wide population in the late 19th and early 20th century was on a mission to connect the world by telephone and improve the user experience.

In the quest to achieve these goals, it did not take long for people to begin experimenting with wireless communications, which would help to free human beings from the phone cords that kept them leashed to their kitchen wall, the desk in their office, and the corner phone booth. These were cords that—no matter how long or flexible—greatly limited our mobility.

With that vision in mind, let's fast forward to 1973—and the debut of the DynaTAC, the prototype of the world's first FCC-approved handheld cellular phone, the DynaTAC 8000x. That year, Dr. Martin Cooper, a general manager for Motorola's Communications Systems Division, who is widely considered to be the inventor of the first portable handset, became the first person to make a call using a portable cellular telephone. (And who did he choose to call? His rival, Dr. Joel Engel, head of research at Bell Labs, of course.)

The prototype phone Cooper used was clunky, wide, and heavy—shaped not unlike a plastic boot with an antenna—and today, looks as outdated as bell-bottoms and mutton-chop sideburns. But in 1973, this thing was cool. More than that, it was a marvel. Keep in mind that cordless telephones had not even been introduced into the market yet.

Now, admittedly, we are skipping over a great deal of telecommunications history that transpired between Bell's achievement and Cooper's and made this important moment in 1973 possible. These transformative events—to name only a few—include the invention of wireless telegraphy, Italian inventor Guglielmo Marconi's first transatlantic radiotelegraph transmission in 1902, and the invention of amplitude-modulated (AM) and frequency-modulated radio (FM).

Long before Cooper placed his call to Engel, people were familiar with wireless, person-to-person communications. Radiotelephones made their debut as a military communications tool in World War I. Even cellular communications, developed by Bell Labs and first introduced into police cars, had been around since just after World War II. (Use of one-way police radio communications dates back even further, to the late 1920s.)

Then there was the development of a little semiconductor device known as the transistor. And when the transistor radio hit the consumer market in the 1950s—particularly the version developed by a new Japanese company known as Sony—it was an instant sensation. Music and information were now pocket-portable, and consumers *loved* it.

Of course, other milestones in technology occurred that had a tremendous impact on communications—such as television, tape recorders, and video recorders. But Cooper's achievement in 1973 is particularly important to the story of mobility. He provided a glimpse into the future of mobile communications on a person-to-person level.

It would take ten years after Cooper made his famous cell phone call for Motorola to introduce its first handheld mobile phone, the DynaTAC 8000x, to the U.S. consumer audience. It was much slimmer than the prototype, but still weighed 28 ounces. (Comparatively, an Apple iPhone 3G weighs just 4.7 ounces.)

The DynaTAC 8000x, as shown in Figure 6-2, provided only one hour of talk time and could store just 30 phone numbers. It also cost approximately $4,000—a price point that immediately defined it as a gee-whiz luxury item or toy for those with disposable income instead of a practical, everyday communication tool within the average person's reach.

Figure 6-2   *Heavy Stuff: Motorola's DynaTAC 8000x*

However, the DynaTAC 8000x did get people thinking about mobility and how this form of communication had the potential to someday change their lives in a meaningful and positive way. "People want to talk to other people—not a house, or an office, or a car. Given a choice, people will demand the freedom to communicate wherever they are, unfettered by the infamous copper wire. It is that freedom we sought to vividly demonstrate in 1973," said Martin Cooper in an April 2003 interview, on the 30th anniversary of that first cell phone call.[3]

But mobile communications is not just about being free; it's about being able to go where you want, when you want, while staying connected to whatever and whoever is important to you. It's about not missing out. "In all of human history, there has been this desire for connectedness," says Richard Tedlow. "Connectedness is like a drug, and once you taste it, you don't want it taken away from you."

That need for connectedness is what drove Henry Ford to build the Model T, says Tedlow. "He grew up on a farm and absolutely loathed rural isolation," he explains. "The Model T, it could be argued, was more than just a transportation device. It was a mobile communication device. It connected people in a way like nothing had before."

Tedlow says "Mobility is also the whole history of computing," adding that the "real turning point in mobile computing" came two years before the world learned it was possible for a person to have a telephone conversation while walking untethered through the streets of New York City.

"In 1971, Intel released the world's first microprocessor, the Intel 4004," he says. "That is what really made mobility possible."

One Chip Makes You Smaller

Before Intel introduced the 4004, "there were no customer-programmable microprocessors on the market. It was the first and it was the enabling technology that propelled software into the limelight as a key player in the world of digital electronics design."[4]

Originally created for use in handheld calculators, the 4-bit microprocessor presented the first central processing unit (CPU) on one chip. It represented four important words in modern computing: small, fast, powerful, and affordable.

This little chip set in motion the "democratization" of computing, according to Tedlow. It allowed for innovation in computer design that would, within only a decade, usher in the era of *personal* computing.

Certainly, computers had been present in the business world for decades prior to the microchip. Enormous computers such as ENIAC (designed by the U.S. military) and UNIVAC (the first commercial computer produced in the United States) needed entire rooms just to house them. And for all the power they consumed, compared to today's computers, they were capable of doing little in the way of computing—and certainly nothing creative.

But most important, until microprocessing changed the landscape, computers were simply not accessible to the "common" person and certainly were not something that had a place in the home.

"In the past, computing was like a priesthood," says Tedlow. "People wearing white jackets would work apart from everyone else in the building, in secure computer rooms. I remember when the Xerox machine was introduced into the office environment. Only select people were allowed to touch it."

The microprocessor caused explosive growth in the development of computers—much smaller computers—and their adoption as everyday business tools. Now, people were more connected to the information they needed to be productive—and, of course, the technology enabled them to work faster and more efficiently. Thus, the microprocessor—along with personal computing—had a tremendous impact on business productivity in the 1970s and 1980s: just more than 1 percent annual growth, which was actually quite significant, back in the day.

By 1981, the first portable computer made its debut. The AC-powered Osborne 1, developed by computer designer Adam Osborne, featured a floppy disk based with 64 K of memory. (See Figure 6-3.) It even had word processing capabilities (WordStar)—never mind that it could display only 40 characters at a time across a screen less than 5 inches wide. The upside: At just $1,795, it was relatively inexpensive for a computer. The big downside: It weighed about 25 pounds. Hence the nickname: The Osborne "luggable."

Figure 6-3   *Lug It or Leave It: The Osborne 1*

Many consider the Osborne to be the first laptop computer, even though it was far from sleek or easy to carry—and was portable only to the extent that it could be taken to and used in places with an electrical outlet. The Osborne's introduction into the marketplace, and its popularity, prompted companies such as IBM, Compaq (which made the first IBM clone), and Zenith to follow with their own luggables and start thinking seriously about portable computing's future.

Luggable computers did little to usher in what we consider today to be our modern era of mobile computing. Even Apple Computer's revolutionary—and lighter—Macintosh 128K with keyboard and mouse, introduced in 1984, was not something you really wanted to carry from place to place on a regular basis (even though some people did proudly cart their Mac between their home and office).

Networked computing is what really changed the game, by providing access to more information and enabling greater connectivity. Laptop computing and VPN technology, which enabled remote working, also had a big impact. From 1996 to 2004, thanks largely to the adoption of network-based computing, U.S. productivity growth hit 3 to 5 percent annually. And although there has been a bit of a lull in productivity in the years since that boom time, according to Cisco CEO John Chambers, we can expect to see significant increases moving forward—perhaps an annual growth rate of 5 percent, thanks to Web 2.0, handheld computing and smartphones in the new "borderless organization." (See Figure 6-4.)

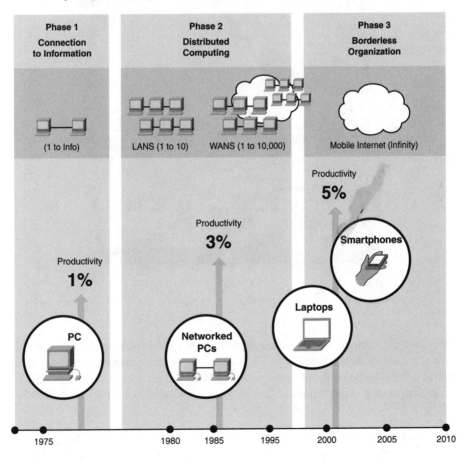

Figure 6-4 *The Productivity Timeline*

Handheld Harvest: Apples to BlackBerrys

In 1993, the minds at Apple—recognizing that personal computing was in a rut, that lug-gables and other PCs were not exactly freeing the masses, and that an evolution was sore-ly needed—introduced the Apple MessagePad. Better known as the Newton, this device had handwriting recognition technology and an array of useful organizational and pro-ductivity tools, as shown in Figure 6-5.

Figure 6-5   *The First PDA: The Apple Newton*

However, although the Newton was indeed innovative and cool, it was also cumbersome for a "handheld" device. Essentially, it was a tablet with a matching stylus and not some-thing you could slip easily into your pocket (that is, without ripping it—or tearing it off completely). And it was expensive. The Newton was kind of like the DynaTAC 8000x of PDAs.

Just a few years later, along came the PalmPilot and other types of PDAs, which became a part of everyday life for many people—seemingly overnight. The first Palm devices were the PalmPilot 1000 and 5000. They featured the pen interface and handwriting recognition pioneered by Apple with its Newton device. But PalmPilots were smaller, sleeker, and more affordable, and by the end of 1996, their first year on the market, 3Com's Palm Computing had sold more than 350,000 units.

Even though print and outdoor advertising for Palm in the late 1990s caused a stir because it featured a naked woman in various (tasteful) poses with the Palm device, it's important to note that this campaign probably had a lot to do with people starting to view handheld mobile devices as seamless extensions of themselves. The campaign was meant to highlight the "beauty" of the PalmPilot's design, but it also made it clear that having a close relationship with one's personal technology was a natural thing.

The PalmPilot's popularity helped put handheld innovation on the fast track. By the late 1990s, a device even more compelling than the PDA would steal the show. It also would create a worldwide following of "addicts"—President Barack Obama, famously, among them. The BlackBerry.

Canada-based Research in Motion (RIM) introduced the BlackBerry (affectionately known by the aforementioned community of BlackBerry addicts as a "CrackBerry") in 1999. The BlackBerry was the first device that could truly "extend the office to the road."[5] An all-in-one wireless data and voice device, Blackberry earned its initial fame with its capability to synchronize company mail systems so that users did not need different email addresses for use when traveling.[6]

Obviously, this was a useful feature that is now of even greater importance—personally and professionally—for many people today worldwide. The BlackBerry's heritage might be in the PDA realm, but today it has a wide range of functions, including touch screens and a workable web browser. BlackBerry is the leader of the ever-growing legion of modern smartphones: Phones doing their best to prove they can deliver like PCs, absolving people of the need to lug around heavy technological baggage.

From early 2004, when approximately 1 million people were using BlackBerrys, usage doubled annually until more than 20 million people worldwide were using the devices. And although this population is growing rapidly, it is still a relatively small percentage of today's knowledge workers—about one in five—who have access to the efficiencies realized by handheld devices such as the BlackBerry. As the penetration moves closer to 100 percent, the impact on the way we conduct business—and secure it—will be profound.

These Unprecedented Times

This evolution, from Bell's liquid transmitter to the transistor to the microprocessor to the Osborne to the BlackBerry, has led to smartphones—and the ability for people to be more productive than ever before. Today's smartphones, such as Apple's revolutionary iPhone and RIM's BlackBerry Storm, enable us to do everything from reading and sending email, accessing web-based enterprise business applications, sending and receiving text, viewing maps and getting directions, keeping calendars, checking stock portfolios, taking photos, watching video clips, playing games, listening to music, and—yes—talking the old-fashioned way, person to person, over the phone.

With so much power and possibility in one small device, it's no wonder we are entranced. But don't think for a moment that our fascination with the smartphone is a flash in the pan. It is more of a cultural shift.

Richard Tedlow says, "This is no fad, although like a fad, it is *fun*. Keep in mind, though, that these two things are not mutually exclusive. Handheld devices are not just increasing productivity—they are redefining it. And people are enjoying it."

He admits that one thing is different about this particular technological revolution, though: It is driven by users. Never before have users demanded—so loudly, adamantly, and in ever-growing numbers—that their employers allow them to bring whatever technology they choose into the enterprise.

"I really can't think of any time in history like this," says Tedlow. But how far away are we from a time when the handheld will replace the laptop in the enterprise? For many people worldwide, a smartphone is already their primary computing device. For some, it's their *only* computing device. This is particularly true in developing countries where it is more efficient for people to access the Internet through a smartphone than to wait for the arrival of broadband.

Without a doubt, the evolving smartphone will be at the center of our always-on, always connected personal and business lives. (Many "CrackBerry" users already understand the impact these devices have on them personally.) But what is less obvious is the effect smartphones and other handheld computing devices, and the new web-centric computing model, will have on global productivity over the next two decades.

Spend some time with a 17 year old. You likely will find that he or she uses a smartphone more often than a PC to engage with friends over Facebook. This trend is an indicator of what is to come in the business world. The next-generation workforce will not only be accustomed to using handheld mobile devices as their go-to communication and productivity tools, but they also will *expect* to use them while on the job. The current workforce is already leaning in that direction: A recent study by IBM found that 50 percent of consumers in China, the United Kingdom, and the United States would substitute their Internet usage on a PC for a mobile device.[7]

It took years for businesses to understand and accept the PC's—and the Internet's—role in business. So, too, did their embracing the idea of employees using a laptop and doing their work remotely. The impact mobile devices will have on business effectiveness, and overall GDP growth in the global economy, cannot be trivialized. (The same is true for the borderless computing model, discussed at the end of this book, and how it will transform companies' security policies.)

As we explore in the following chapters, the widespread adoption of handheld computing will be driven by a push and a pull: Organizations will pull it into their businesses to gain competitive advantage, and workers will push it into the enterprise because of their computing experiences in the consumer world.

Evolution of the Smartphone

The preeminence of the smartphone as a business computing platform is a function of the capabilities of the platform. iPhone users have had a taste of a handheld device with the power of a general purpose operating system. With a few more advancements of the technical components of the smartphone, it is easy to see how this form factor will overtake other computing platforms in importance.

The top-level component of the smartphone is the operating system. Symbian, as of early 2009, held market leadership of the smartphone operating system market, followed by BlackBerry, according to Infonetics Research—and Apple's iPhone OS X was not far behind.[8] Meanwhile, open-source platforms such as Google Android have been gaining more traction, particularly since the T-Mobile G1 "Google phone" made its debut in September 2008 and has since been marketed heavily to Gen Y users.

The Android open-source model is still a bit of a wildcard right now but could fundamentally shift the economics of the smartphone industry over time. Admittedly, the G1 has not achieved the same popularity as the iPhone, although more than 1 million units were shipped between October 2008 and August 2009.[9] And other leading developers, including the Motorola/Verizon partnership around the "Moto," are introducing new mobile phones featuring this platform. Regardless of whether the Android model becomes a formidable competitor to established leaders in the smartphone space, however, it can be said that *all* these devices are pushing the pace of development in the handheld mobile device category.

After the operating system, the next major building block of the smartphone is the network connection: Wireless industry research firm NPD Group reports that as of early 2009, two-thirds of smartphones now use 3G networks, compared to just 46 percent the year before.[10] Some experts expect that the spread of 3G Long Term Evolution (LTE)—essentially, 4G, and which many traditional wireless telecom companies are backing—and mobile WiMAX (which, as of the latter half of 2009, was available in approximately 40 U.S. cities) will eventually lead mobile operators to move to an "open" access, any client device, connected Internet model.

Meanwhile, enhancements in wireless fidelity (WiFi) technology are expected to make a tremendous, positive impact on the smartphone-as-PC experience—and it's already giving cell phone providers some stiff competition. WiFi, when present, enables the "always connected" experience and typically enables users to download data at speeds much faster than what their cell phone provider offers. The cost of adding WiFi capability to a consumer device has dropped to near zero, meaning waves of new consumer products will be shipping with WiFi, further spreading the use of WiFi hotspots as a network access mechanism, and smartphones will take full advantage of this connection medium.

However, despite these advancements, still a few building blocks of the smartphone need to evolve before twilight really starts to cast a shadow on the traditional laptop, according to Brett Galloway, senior vice president of the Cisco Wireless, Security, and Routing Technology Group. "Battery life, cost, and size," he says. "Right now, these are three major constraints."

As for cost and size, those things will naturally decrease over time, as has been the case with devices since the dawn of electronic communication and computing. Just look at today's netbook—also known as the "mini notebook" computer—which provides a rich computing and multimedia experience but on a light, compact, and energy-efficient device. It's also a low-cost computing option: $300 to $400, or even less, for a netbook with much of the same functionality as a basic PC.

Even though netbooks, at first, did not seem as though they had the potential to "fundamentally [change] the way PCs are used...the idea of inexpensive, portable PC-equivalents" is definitely catching on.[11] Netbooks were initially designed primarily for people who wanted a nice, affordable computer to check email and surf the Web. But the netbook is no longer just a low-cost computing option for the casual user: Professionals and students are using netbooks to cost-effectively enhance their efficiency, productivity, and mobility, which is why they are pushing and paying for better performance from these computers. (And why they are expecting more from their smartphones, as well.) Major chip vendors, such as Qualcomm with its "snapdragon" chipset, will continue to push the price performance curve of netbooks even further.

According to Deloitte, netbooks represented the fastest-growing PC segment in 2009.[12] And market research firm iSuppli Corp. predicts that shipments of low-cost netbook PC displays will nearly quadruple between 2008 and 2012 (reaching 47.4 million units) as consumer demand soars even higher for inexpensive, small form-factor PCs.[13] Netbooks, smartphones, and tablet computers are among the plethora of new devices that will change the way we think about business computing.

Meanwhile, there remains the question of power. As Cisco's Brett Galloway says, battery life needs to improve before handheld devices can truly deliver an experience that rivals the laptop. The good news is that companies are making strides with improving battery life for handheld devices, so expect things to change rapidly on this front in the near future.

For instance, Sony Corp. has been working to enhance the power and extend the lifespan of lithium ion batteries. Its rechargeable olivine-type lithium ion phosphate batteries introduced in 2009 can rejuice fast (almost completely, in just 30 minutes) and provides four times the capacity of other batteries. Right now, these batteries are meant for power tools, but it's expected they will soon be used to power mobile devices such as laptops and smartphones.[14]

The final area in which smartphones need to improve is display efficiency and quality. Some companies are already looking to move away from conventional liquid crystal display (LCD) panels and toward active-matrix organic light-emitting diode (AM-OLED) technology. Manufacturers such as Nokia and Samsung offer this technology in their costlier smartphone models. (AM-OLED is 50 to 80 percent more expensive than conventional LCD screens, an obvious clue as to why they are not yet being mass-produced.[15])

AM-OLED technology resides in a thin layer of organic materials that enables screens to glow on their own: The result, slimmer screens that use less power, boast faster response speed, and have more vivid colors. Of course, it will likely be a long time before LCD screens lose their dominance in the marketplace, but expect to see a steady increase in the efficiency and fidelity of handheld displays over the next few years.

Handheld computing does need to evolve further before it can largely replace the laptop computing experience. But if you consider the progress these devices have made from the clunky DynaTac 8000x of four decades ago to today's iPhone 3G, it's not hard to imagine that in the next three to five years, many of us will be doing the majority of our business computing on a handheld mobile device—making the traditional laptop not extinct, but less important.

The evolution of the smartphone is not just a story about another neat gizmo becoming a part of our everyday lives. It marks the beginning of a transformation in the way we interact with business information. From a historical perspective, the smartphone and the mobile Internet have the potential to drive wave after wave of increasing productivity and competitive advantage for forward-thinking companies that can harness the power and possibility of these technological innovations.

So, just like Martin Cooper and the DynaTac 8000x in 1973, when you hold today's smartphone, you hold the future in your hand.

Endnotes

[1] "Inventing the Telephone," AT&T corporate website. http://www.corp.att.com/history/inventing.html.

[2] Ibid.

[3] "30 Years of Wireless Voice Communications Have Paved the Way for the Wireless Internet, says Cooper," ArrayComm, media release, April 3, 2003. http://www.thefreelibrary.com/Inventor+and+ArrayComm+CEO+Martin+Cooper+ Celebrates+30th+Anniversary...-a099558362.

[4] "Intel's First Microprocessor—the Intel 4004." http://www.intel.com/museum/archives/4004.htm.

[5] "ZDNet: Definition for: BlackBerry," ZDNet.com. http://dictionary.zdnet.com/definition/BlackBerry.html.

[6] Ibid.

[7] "50% Say They'd Substitute Mobile Web for PC, Says IBM Study," Wireless and Mobile News, October 23, 2008. http://www.wirelessandmobilenews.com/2008/10/50_say_theyd_substitute_mobile_web_ for_pc_says_ibm_study.html.

[8] "Smartphone sales buck recession," media release, March 26, 2009. http://www.infonetics.com/pr/2009/2h08-mobile-wifi-phones-market-research-highlights.asp.

[9] "The Google Android Opportunity: Follow Apple's iPhone," Google Watch (eWeek blog), by Clint Boulton, August 17, 2009. http://googlewatch.eweek.com/content/hello_android/the_google_android_opportunity_follow_apples_iphone.html.

[10] "The NPD Group: Despite Recession, U.S. Smartphone Market is Growing," The NPD Group, media release, March 3, 2009. http://www.npd.com/press/releases/press_090303.html.

[11] "Disrupting the PC: the rise of the netbook," Deloitte Technology Predictions 2009. http://www.deloitte.co.uk/TMTPredictions/technology/Disrupting-the-PC-the-rise-of-the-netbook.cfm.

[12] Ibid.

[13] "Rapid growth seen in netbook LCD shipments," EE Times, April 6, 2009. http://www.eetimes.com/news/latest/showArticle.jhtml;jsessionid=QIUR4ZMAOU2RRQE1GHPSKHWATMY32JVN?articleID=216403088&printable=true&printable=true.

[14] "Sony's latest Olivine-type lithium iron Battery—4X Bigger Capacity than Regular Battery," Tech News, August 12, 2009. http://www.hardwaresphere.com/2009/08/12/sony-latest-olivine-type-lithium-iron-battery/.

[15] "Smartphone battle opens door for new OLED Technology," By Rhee So-eui and Sinead Carew, Reuters India, August 14, 2009. http://in.reuters.com/article/technologyNews/idINIndia-41756520090814.

References

AntiqueTelephoneHistory.com. http://www.antiquetelephonehistory.com/liquid2.html.

Apple Computer, Inc., website. http://www.apple.com.

"Cisco CEO John Chambers on Speeding Up Innovation," *BusinessWeek*, "Next Innovation Tools & Trends" blog posting by Matt Vella, September 28, 2009. http://www.businessweek.com/innovate/next/archives/2008/09/cisco_ceo_john.html.

Computer History Museum. http://www.computerhistory.org/.

"Interop '07: Cisco's John Chambers sees Web 2.0 driving major productivity gains," TechRepublic.com, "Tech Sanity Check" blog, posting by Jason Hiner, May 2, 2007. http://blogs.techrepublic.com.com/hiner/?p=482.

"March 10, 1876: 'Mr. Watson, Come Here...'" By Randy Alfred, *Wired* magazine, March 10, 2008. http://www.wired.com/science/discoveries/news/2008/03/dayintech_0310.

Palm USA website. www.palm.com.

RIM website. http://www.rim.com/.

The Osborne 1, EconomicExpert.com.
http://www.economicexpert.com/a/Osborne:1.htm.

Transistor Radios, PBS website.
http://www.pbs.org/transistor/background1/events/tradio.html.

"Used Radio Phones to Direct Air Fighters; Squadrons of Our Airplanes Were
Maneuvered from Ground During Last War Days," *The New York Times*, November 15,
1918. http://query.nytimes.com/mem/archive-
free/pdf?_r=1&res=940DE7DB1239E13ABC4E52DFB7678383609EDE.

Chapter 7

The Consumerization of IT

This chapter includes the following topics:

- Talkin' 'bout an Evolution

- Blame It on the Music

- More Than Just Smartphones

- Consumerization: A Pull and a Push

- Safely Consumerizing IT

The phrase "I want my MTV" defined a generation part Gen X, part Gen Y. Now, that same group—all grown-up and entrenched in the workforce—is shouting out another demand ignited not just by personal desire, but also the want and need for greater productivity and connectivity in all aspects of their lives: "I want my iPhone."

This growing chorus—that includes the voices of many others on both sides of the MTV Generation, those born between 1975 and 1986—signals a major shift toward the consumerization of IT. And this movement will have a profound impact on the future of enterprise computing and security.

In the enterprise, there is growing demand for the acceptance of new computing tools—both hardware and applications—that first gain their popularity in the consumer space before being pulled into the business organization (or *pushed*, as IT often views it) by employees. Industry analysts generally recognize this trend as the consumerization of IT.

The implications of this trend are significant: a better, more efficient computing experience for end users and dramatically lowered costs for the enterprise. This means that everyone wins, right? So, what's not to like?

Well, for any enterprise today facing pressure from the consumerization of IT, the top-of-mind issue is security. How can the organization protect users and their data when the endpoint becomes uncontrolled? This is a significant challenge, and one that must be solved—quickly—because the wave of consumerization in the business world cannot be prevented. And it is counterproductive for companies to continue to resist.

Talkin' 'bout an Evolution

Right now, what's accelerating the consumerization of IT is the smartphone. As we learned in the previous chapter, handheld devices are becoming increasingly powerful, driven by advances in battery power density, processor performance, and display efficiency and fidelity. Many mobile users conclude that the 8-pound-or-so burden they lug around now—the laptop computer—can be left at home or the office more often.

It is not unreasonable to project that within five years the smartphone could become the primary computing tool for the mobile user, and also, in the borderless enterprise—that all users will be mobile users. Will a smartphone replace a traditional PC? Not entirely. But as the capabilities of a smartphone rapidly increase, the amount of time a person must spend working on a traditional laptop or desktop decreases. Thus, the importance of the smartphone—and the security scheme that protects it— will grow over time.

Apple's iPhone is an iconic device in this evolution because it introduced the first really usable web browser on a handheld device, a pivotal step toward the smartphone becoming a primary enterprise computing device. "What's interesting about the iPhone, in terms of the consumerization of IT trend, is that it has finally moved from being a cell phone with a browser to a computing device that also makes phone calls," says Brett Galloway, senior vice president of the Cisco Wireless, Security, and Routing Technology Group.

He continues, "The iPhone is not just a consumer product. It's a platform. That's the way it is built: Whatever the platform is, people build on top of it. We've seen this happen before. This is why the CD-ROM took off as a format—because of the popularity of audio CDs in the consumer market. Whatever drives consumer volume ends up being the technology platform."

However, before the tipping point is actually reached and consumers are ready to make a wholesale shift to handheld devices for most or all of their communication and computing needs, Chris Christiansen, program vice president for IDC's security products and services group, anticipates continued evolution of the laptop and the smartphone over the next few years. "The laptop will get smaller, while the smartphone likely will get somewhat bigger," he says. "More importantly, the smartphone will become more intelligent, secure, and manageable and able to process local and network data in a much more granular way."

It's true that worldwide, many people are already using their handheld device as the go-to tool of choice—or necessity—for work and play. Or at least, they're trying to, even if the technology to fully support their preference from a security—and cultural—standpoint is not yet there. "You could say this movement has already happened in the Asia-Pacific region and in Europe," says Christiansen. "People are transacting and using their mobile devices, particularly their smartphones, for a wide variety of consumer and business applications. There has been considerable 'graying' of business and consumer use outside of the United States."

Businesses and educational institutions of all types are eager to contain this movement—this infiltration of consumer technology undermining the fortifications designed to keep the organization's network and data secure. The problem is amplified by the increasingly loud and unified voice of consumers demanding that the technology *they* choose be permitted and supported, regardless of whether adequate security technology and policies exist. It's as if today, more than 20 years after it first aired, Apple's famous "1984" TV ad introducing the Macintosh PC to the world has become even more relevant: But instead of a sledgehammer shattering the status quo and freeing the masses from the constraints of what is considered "safe" by the establishment, it's a smartphone that is setting us free.

So, are consumers becoming more passionate about their handheld devices because of the convenience of these increasingly affordable tools and their ability to significantly enhance productivity and connectivity? That's only part of the story. Although those factors might be what made the laptop the modern day briefcase that moves relatively seamlessly between the worlds of "work" and "home," truly understanding why handheld devices like smartphones are transforming personal and business computing requires digging deeper into the human psyche. The affinity a growing population of consumers is feeling toward their handheld devices is not just about what they can do with them, but also what they say about who they are.

Blame It on the Music

Sony's introduction and savvy marketing of the portable cassette player, The Walkman, in 1979 made two key contributions to the consumerization of IT trend of today: First, it gave people a taste of always-on, always-ready access to content. In this case, their content was their music—an inherently personal type of content. Second, it allowed individuals to just put on their headphones and "tune out" the world around them whenever and wherever they pleased. The Walkman was all about personal choice and mobility.

Fast forward to 2001: The launch of Apple's iPod. The ad campaigns used to introduce the first iPod and sell its various incarnations since haven't been about the wonders of mobility, although that certainly has been implied. Even the always-advancing technology of the portable media player itself has often been a secondary message. The ads, by and large, are about iPods as a form of personal expression—and their capability to deliver a highly personalized listening, and now also viewing, experience. From the vibrant range of colors of iPod shells to the ubiquitous shadow silhouettes of joyful, frenetically dancing people gracing billboards and bus shelters around the globe, the message is clear: An iPod is a reflection of the user. The two are deeply intertwined.

Meanwhile, mobile phones and other handheld devices are not immune to users' deep-seated desire to make the technology they constantly touch and carry around in their pocket uniquely and comfortably theirs. This need has spawned an entire industry that manufactures cases, "skins," charms, stickers, and other "bling" for the sole purpose of handheld device decoration. And don't forget ringtones: Even the way a mobile device sounds off to the world is often of great personal importance to users. From the image displayed on the device's screen to the music, games, and applications a user puts into it, handheld devices exist for communication, computing *and* personal expression.

"Handheld devices today are like jewelry," says Rebecca Jacoby, senior vice president and chief information officer for Cisco. "There has to be some kind of glamour aspect to them. What you decide to keep close to you is a real personal choice. It's an aspect of you."

Therefore, the fact that so many users have tremendous difficulty—and outright resistance to—completely putting aside or severely restricting what they view as a part of themselves for 8 or more hours a day, 5 days a week, just to help their employer—and IT department—sleep better at night, should not be a surprise.

Keep His BlackBerry? Yes, He Can.   President Barack Obama is perhaps the most high-profile "CrackBerry" addict in the world. But after winning the U.S. presidential election in 2008, he was informed he would probably have to give up his beloved BlackBerry because of the security risks it posed. Additional complications: A president's emails can be subpoenaed by the U.S. Congress and courts, and the Presidential Records Act of 1978 makes a president's correspondence, which today includes email, part of the official record and, therefore, available for public review.

Although his predecessor, George W. Bush, officially swore off personal email use before his first inauguration nearly a decade before, letting go of the 24/7 connectivity of the BlackBerry that he was so accustomed to would not be such an easy choice for Mr. Obama. Especially because his new administration—just as his presidential campaign did—relies heavily on the Internet and Web 2.0 tools to communicate regularly with the masses. Insisting that the man in the Oval Office be completely disengaged from his Blackberry device would be incongruous.

So, Mr. Obama pushed back, making it clear that "the enterprise" would need to accommodate his technology preference. And he won the fight—sort of. He is allowed to keep in touch with senior staff and a select group of family and friends with a BlackBerry featuring souped-up security. The president might not like such restrictions on his personal and business communication, but no doubt it's more desirable than the alternative—giving up his handheld device altogether. And so, the consumerization of IT brought change to The White House in 2009.

More Than Just Smartphones

The trend toward the consumerization of IT is clearly propelled by the deep personal connection users have with their handheld devices. But this affinity is not reserved for smartphones. Users are often just as passionate about their choice of laptop or desktop machine. This is exemplified by the growing use of Apple laptops and desktops in many types of businesses—and not just those categorized as "creative."

Many users prefer to use an Apple at work because it is the same operating system they use at home. Or it might be that the technical staff prefers the UNIX core of the Apple, or possibly Linux as a desktop. In addition to the choice of operating system, you have an infinite array of choices of hardware configurations. Some people, for example, might want an "ultralight" laptop, whereas others prefer a full-featured model. And for some users, their work might require a large desktop with multiple processors and hardware graphics accelerators.

A wide range of computing devices on the market can suit a user's particular work and personal needs. People have become accustomed to having so much choice as consumers that they are increasingly looking for the same flexibility within the enterprise. Often, this desire for choice of computing devices is more than just a whim: The "fit" of computing tools has a direct impact on an end user's productivity.

Consumerization is not just about devices, either. Web 2.0 applications in the consumer world are also pulled into the enterprise. Millions of users rely on social networking sites such as Facebook, LinkedIn, and Twitter or web-based applications such as Google Docs to communicate and to organize their personal and professional lives. For many enterprises, use of these sites and applications by employees are pushing the boundaries of security policies to their limits—daily.

The question organizations are struggling with is whether their employees should be allowed to use these applications—especially because they do seem to enhance productivity. If the answer is yes, then what tools exist that can filter and control the flow of sensitive data via these applications? Many companies are struggling with the ambiguities of Web 2.0 usage. (See Chapter 13, "Collaboration Without Confidence.") Many outright block it, fully realizing their decision likely has a costly business impact—if not now, then eventually. Other organizations do allow it, but worry constantly about security vulnerabilities or a lack of regulatory compliance.

Whether they embrace it or resist it today, most enterprise customers recognize that they need a proactive security policy to deal—realistically—with the surge of devices and applications flooding into the enterprise from the consumer realm. Most IT organizations resist these changes simply because they cause change—and change implies new costs and risks. But this mind-set is changing, too, and it could make the consumerization of IT rip through the enterprise at an astonishing pace.

Consumerization: A Pull and a Push

Most use of consumer devices in the enterprise is the result of end user "pull"—such as when an executive wants to start using iPhones because of her personal preference, or when a department starts exchanging information via Google Docs because it's convenient and easy. Control- and protection-minded IT departments typically resist the pull—which they view as an unwelcome and uncomfortable initiative from employees—because with it they see yet another platform that must be supported, along with additional costs and risks.

But an intriguing potential trade-off exists here: Imagine if the benefit of consumerized IT was so valuable to end users that they would be willing to participate more actively in the provisioning and support of enterprise computing? At Cisco, it's already happening, and recent work done internally suggests that the consumerization of IT might actually *lower* IT support costs, possibly by a significant amount.

The Cisco Global Technical Response Center (GTRC) supports more than 67,000 users and 30,000 contractors on six continents. Supporting the computing needs of this immense global workforce is a significant undertaking. So, when the company decided it was time to respond to increasing employee demand to allow Apple's Mac computers into the enterprise, the Cisco IT team determined that the best way to connect with the employee community would be through Web 2.0 applications.

"We set up a communication module, like a Mac wiki, that essentially says, 'If you're thinking about getting a Mac or an iPhone, here are the plusses and minuses,'" says Cisco senior vice president and CIO Rebecca Jacoby. "And we just let people participate in that environment and make their own decisions. This has been a really different style of operation for IT."

The Cisco IT team has seen rewards for its use of Web 2.0 technologies and flexibility about allowing new devices into the enterprise. "A year ago, we had no unsolicited remarks from employees about how we were doing, or what we could do better. Zero. Now, we have something like 12 percent telling us they think we are doing a good job," says Jacoby. "One of the significant jump points was when we actually announced that employees could get a Mac. We hadn't even gotten the Macs yet, but employees were just happy knowing they *could* have one."

After the successful introduction of the Mac into the enterprise, the Cisco decision to allow other devices did come with a catch, according to Jacoby. "We told people they had to pay for the devices themselves, or that they could have only a partial stipend," she says. "But the interesting thing is that we have received no flak whatsoever from employees for telling them they have to pay for these devices. Nor have we received any flak for going to a community self-support model."

"Everyone is unhappy with the device that you select for them," says Rami Mazid, vice president, IT-Global Client Services and Operations for Cisco. "So, if you let them choose their own device, their satisfaction—and productivity—will be higher. At Cisco, we have found that users are actually willing to be self-supported in exchange for this flexibility."

The community self-support model Cisco recently introduced is also lowering support costs significantly for the organization, according to Mazid. He says the average case requiring GTRC support could be reduced from about $20 to $12. And of the 181,000 unique cases GTRC was asked to provide support for in the first quarter of fiscal year 2009, Mazid says 38,000 could have been resolved through the self-support model. So, as more people make use of self-services and community support, the cost savings will grow for Cisco.

The experience of Cisco GTRC's self-support model and the introduction of the Mac into the enterprise are profound. If the consumerization of IT can translate to lower costs for the organization—and produce better end user satisfaction—the trend will be fully unleashed. IT departments can see this as a way to conserve their precious resources and can begin to push these types of programs. And with a push from IT and a pull from delighted end users, the consumerization of IT can be rapid and unstoppable.

The data suggests that within a few years, the model of enterprise computing will change dramatically. Today, the typical enterprise has a few "standard issue" computing platforms—desktop, laptop, smartphone. (And you have your choice of color, as long as it is black.) The enterprise is like the government that mandates three establishment-approved outfits that all citizens must wear. But people want to be people, and they certainly do not want to wear a drab uniform. Likewise, they want choice in the computing tools they use.

Tomorrow, end users will procure a phone and a laptop from whatever source they want—maybe it's through the company or maybe it's from Best Buy. Some will have a company stipend, and some will simply furnish their own machines. Regardless of the tool selected, the user can provision the system and engage the corporate network on their own. They can have a better computing experience, at a lower cost to the corporation. It's a powerful concept and one that appears to be before us.

However, to make this vision of the consumerized IT experience into a reality, some significant tools are needed.

Safely Consumerizing IT

The idea behind the consumerization of IT is that tomorrow's computing devices are becoming more fashion-oriented—just like jewelry. Part and parcel with that trend is the recognition that consumers need to mix business and pleasure, or at least, business and personal computing.

In tomorrow's workplace, trying to prevent a blend of business and personal computing will be impractical and incredibly inefficient. It would be like asking employees to walk to the corner store to use a payphone instead of calling home from their desk to let their family know they will be staying late at the office. The fact is, business users are already blending personal and business computing. So, the question really becomes: How does the company do it safely?

Desktop virtualization is a big part of the answer. It is a powerful tool that helps business and personal computing coexist on a single device. The concept is that consumers can have any device they want—a smartphone or a laptop, in any color and with any configuration—and can connect to the Internet in any way they please for personal use. But when the time comes to access company data, they must switch to a virtual desktop.

Inside the virtual workspace, corporate policies are rigorously and constantly enforced. Every connection on or off the device is scanned, logged, and analyzed to ensure adherence to corporate policy. Data stored on the device may well have disk encryption and other protective measures around it. The enterprise computing space is clean and clearly defined.

When users need to do their personal computing, they would switch out of the corporate computing virtual desktop and back to their personal computing environment. There, they have their own rules, policies, and protections in place.

The virtual machine (VM) creates a vital dividing line between business and personal data and policy. Although this is a powerful concept, it is well understood that reaching a point where virtual desktops can run on the myriad emerging smartphones is probably five years away. However, there is a series of meaningful steps that must be taken on the path to that destination. The convergence of SSL VPN technology, advanced web security scanning, and hybrid-hosted security solutions are making the coexistence of business and personal computing and the consumerization of IT a reality for many companies today.

But again, virtualization is only one facet of security in the Web 2.0 world. Also required is technology that can defend against—and quickly detect—attacks from criminals who create, deploy, and profit from highly sophisticated malware. Development—and enforcement—of realistic policies outlining acceptable use of devices and applications for employees are also key components. And a data loss prevention program that helps to protect an organization's most important, sensitive data from slipping out of the enterprise—accidently or intentionally—is essential.

References

"Half a Billion Mobile TV Viewers and Subscribers in 2013," ABI Research, February 10, 2009. http://www.abiresearch.com/press/1366-Half+a+Billion+Mobile+TV+Viewers+and+Subscribers+in+2013.

Apple "1984" TV ad. http://www.youtube.com/watch?v=R706isyDrqI.

"In Barack Obama's White House, his Blackberry is his VIP," By Christi Parsons and Jim Puzzanghera, Chicago Tribune, January 22, 2009. http://archives.chicagotribune.com/2009/jan/22/science/chi-090122-obama-keeps-blackberry.

"Obama's new Blackberry: The NSA's secure PDA?" by Declan McCullagh, CNET News, January 13, 2009. http://news.cnet.com/obamas-new-blackberry-the-nsas-secure-pda/.

Chapter 8

The Bad Guys from Outside: Malware

This chapter includes the following topics:

- Modern Malware Overview

- Finding the Weak Points

- Social Engineering for Success

- Spamming and Phishing Get Targeted

- Profit Motive

Along with acceptable use policies (AUP) and data loss prevention (DLP), malware, or malicious software, is one of the three critical areas that enterprise security policies must address. Malware is pervasive, painful, and expensive to detect and block.

Malware has been part of computing for decades. In the 1990s, it got onto your computer or network when you stuck an infected floppy disk into your drive, or when a clever hacker gained access to your network. Then, with email becoming more prevalent, hackers designed malware to spread as infected email attachments. Today, the Internet is a fantastic distribution mechanism for malware.

In this chapter, you can find out how malware works and why it presents such a threat to the enterprise. In addition, you learn about the newest sophisticated tactics that malware creators use to trick computer users into downloading their wares.

Modern Malware Overview

Malware, which is malicious software that infiltrates computers, networks, and mobile devices, is part of life in the information age. Malware is sent via email, spreads via portable media storage and drives—such as CDs, USB drives, and MP3 players—and can secretly download onto your computer from websites you trust.

Today, the primary distribution mechanism for malware is the World Wide Web. Malware is served not only from entirely malicious, fraudulent websites but also legitimate websites that have been compromised.

One way in which malware has changed over time is that it's a lot smarter and harder to detect than before. This makes it very difficult to get it out of your systems after they are infected. But malware still depends on vulnerabilities in technology—and weaknesses in human nature—to infiltrate computers and networks.

And hackers aren't trying to get malware onto your computers just for fun, or to see how far they can spread the code they wrote. Modern malware is a for-profit, big-business undertaking. Online criminals invest significant amounts of money and time in more efficient malware and better malware distribution mechanisms because they know the financial rewards can be enormous.

Types of Malware

The original email–propagated viruses, such as the circa-2000 Melissa or I Love You viruses, did not do much besides slow down the performance of your computer and your network. They soaked up bandwidth and processing power by sending copies of themselves to millions of people. This type of malware was created primarily to enable its authors to show off their "development" skills. For David Smith of New Jersey, the author of the Melissa virus, the erstwhile use of his computer skills backfired; following a tip from an AOL employee to law enforcement, Smith ended up spending 20 months in prison.

Following the success of these earlier mass-mailer viruses, a new class of malware was born. This malware, or *spyware*, was used to deliver pop-up ads. A full spectrum of pop-up ad malware exists, ranging from the legitimate but annoying to the illegitimate and harmful.

A good example of legitimate but annoying spyware is the pop-up ad generators (also called adware) often embedded in peer-to-peer applications, such as Kazaa. Users downloading the desired application had to agree to install the adware, but the adware was virtually impossible to remove. Many other pop-up generators and tracking cookies are loaded onto a user's PC without their knowledge, creating annoying ads and capturing personal web browsing information to help target more unwanted advertising.

Other forms of malware are more hostile. A particularly ugly variant of malware, known as *ransomware*, shuts down functionality of the end user device unless the victim pays a ransom. In 2008, several kinds of malware and ransomware for mobile phones showed up in Asia, where workers are more likely to have a mobile phone than a personal computer. As VNUnet reported, when the mobile phone was infected, the phone's owner would receive a message instructing them to pay to restore the phone's functionality.[1]

In a classic scam, a lot of computer-based ransomware masquerades as *anti*spyware or *anti*virus software. It pretends to scan your computer for malware, tells you your device is infected, and asks you to fork over money to access the "full" version of the software that can remove the "found" infections. In 2008, a family of fake antivirus software, known as XP Antivirus, infected millions of computers netting the criminals millions of dollars.

Keylogging malware tracks every keystroke you make and sends the information back to online criminals so that they can use or resell your login names, passwords, credit card numbers, and other useful personal or corporate information.

Rootkits gain access to the core of your operating system and let criminals control your computer or network as administrators. (Some of the fake antimalware products partake in these activities instead of, or as well as, demanding money to "clean" your computer.) After criminals infiltrate your computer, they want to use it to profit. To do so, they make it part of a *botnet*, which is a network of thousands of infected computers that carry out the orders of online criminals by sending out massive amounts of spam, hosting websites, or participating in attacks on websites that are designed to deny visitors access to the sites (also known as a denial of service attack). This type of malware can also turn these websites into malware redirect hubs.

Another technique used by criminals is to create malicious software that looks for a flaw in the browser code or, more often, a flaw in a browser plug-in such as the Flash player. The malware creates a buffer overflow. This is one of the most common and dangerous vulnerabilities; malware piles extra data into a program's buffer or temporary data storage area. Rather than rejecting the extra data, the vulnerable software enables the extra data to be written to the next operation. A carefully crafted exploit can ensure the extra data is an attack vector, which is written to an overflow area that executes the attack. The most common exploits today target web browsers or browser plug-ins such as the Flash player or Adobe Reader. In this case, the victims merely visit a website and can be exploited and have malware installed on their computer without their interaction or knowledge; this is known as a *drive-by download.*

A 2008 Google study of drive-by downloads indicated that more than 3 million URLs on the Internet were found to initiate drive-by downloads. And 1.3 percent of incoming search queries to Google brought up at least one malicious URL in the search results.[2]

Botnets

Botnets are the backbone of criminal activity on the Internet today, and they keep growing in number and sophistication. Internet experts have likened botnets to a pandemic, and say that at one time, up to 25 percent of all Internet-connected computers were part of a botnet.[3] With the steady rollout of broadband infrastructure and unprotected PCs in the emerging economies of the world, the supply of botnets appears unlimited.

Usually, the computer owner won't even know the computer is part of a botnet except for occasional slowdowns in performance. The malware that turns the computer into a botnet node, or "zombie," often invisibly downloads in the background while the computer user innocently surfs the Web. It can also be very clever at hiding from antivirus software, with code that changes every so often (making it harder to identify) or goes dormant for a while (making it harder to find).

Even Trusted Sites Can't Be Trusted

A recent development in malware distribution is the infection of legitimate websites—in enormous numbers—so they start serving up malware. The advantage for malware creators: These sites have been around for a long time, have a good reputation, and are trusted by large numbers of site visitors and security solutions—so they might be easier to exploit.

Modern malware has managed to penetrate the websites of media organizations and publications such as *BusinessWeek*,[4] major companies, government organizations, banks, and online social networks. This enables criminals to take advantage of the millions of visitors to these trusted sites without having the inconvenience and expense of building appealing malware-distributing websites of their own.

In these cases, online criminals attack millions of legitimate websites looking for weaknesses. If they find a vulnerable site, they insert small bits of code, called iFrames, on these trusted webpages so that they start sending visitors to websites that host malware. The iFrame codes make it possible to embed one HTML document inside another one. For instance, the banner ad found on a webpage is often hosted by a different web server than the main content. Online criminals can simply incorporate a malicious URL somewhere in the iFrame, or they can hide it with JavaScript.

How do online criminals get their malicious iFrame onto a legitimate website? Most often, they use SQL injections.

This technique exploits a vulnerability in the database layer of certain web applications and servers. When website developers don't properly sanitize the data transmitted in user input fields (such as forms and user logins) on webpages that use SQL, criminals can take advantage of this weakness to take control of the website and turn it into a malware redirection hub.

Finding the Weak Points

To gain a foothold on your computer and in your corporate network, malware exploits weak points, or vulnerabilities, in widely used technologies. The myriad rapidly developing applications that make up the Web provide a wealth of vulnerabilities for online criminals to exploit.

The Web is made up of billions of pages created by different people with different levels of technical skills, offering rich content in many different formats. Accessing some of this content requires helper applications, such as media players. Many different types of back-end software serve up these webpages and content. And many of those formats, applications, and tools have weaknesses hackers can exploit.

Hackers also can exploit the Web's core infrastructure and basic standards. Many of the standards and much of the infrastructure the Web runs on were designed long before anyone thought of today's amazingly wide-ranging uses of the Web. For example, e-commerce, online banking, online social networking, and enterprise-level cloud-based computing are all common on the Web today. Ideally, you want to feel secure while engaging in those activities. But in the early days, decisions about the Internet and Web's standards and infrastructure heavily emphasized improving connectivity and access to content rather than walling off content in easily securable chunks. So, underlying infrastructure vulnerabilities, along with vulnerabilities in higher-level applications, remain a concern.

Hackers use these vulnerabilities to create exploits that let them penetrate your computer or network. Often, when you visit an infected webpage or open an infected email, the attack code starts snooping around for any known weaknesses in your system.

The malware found on a malicious website—such as one involved in an iFrame attack— begins a series of probes, looking for unpatched weaknesses in your browser, the myriad browser plug-ins you might have installed, your operating system, or any applications you might have running.

The level of sophistication is remarkable in that the malware sites can actually identify the particulars of your computer and operating system and infect or attack the system appropriately. For instance, if you run Safari as your browser, the malware sites won't bother trying any known Internet Explorer vulnerabilities. Instead, they focus on Safari or Safari plug-in weaknesses.

When a useful vulnerability is found, the goal of the malware attack is to create a buffer overflow condition in your computer. This then gives the malware the capability to initiate the download of harmful code—the keyloggers, botnet software, spyware ad generators, or other malware previously discussed.

Malware doesn't only exploit vulnerabilities in technologies. Malware creators and distributors also take advantage of "weaknesses" in human nature, such as curiosity, trust, desire for connection, and carelessness, to dupe users into handing over the keys to their system security.

Social Engineering for Success

To distribute malware, send spam, and acquire sensitive information by posing as a trusted source (also called *phishing*), online criminals increasingly take advantage of human nature to get victims to open an email, visit a website, or give up information. They use sophisticated social engineering techniques, and they hijack reputations of trusted websites and email senders to get their message or malware into your system.

For example, they appear to offer useful Web 2.0 tools, cool games, or interesting news content. When you click the link in the email and visit the site, the site often appears normal. However, in the background it's probing your machine, searching for a vulnerability that lets it install malware on your computer.

Other attacks try to appear like a legitimate bank or commerce site in hopes of capturing your username and password—phishing for your information. Other forms of malware sites try to get you to "buy" something from the site, giving the criminals your credit card information.

In Figure 8-1, we contrast an image of the legitimate ticketing website for the Beijing 2008 Summer Olympics with a scam ticketing website. Oddly enough, the scam site was much better looking and more user-intuitive than the real ticketing site, with better graphics and navigation—which meant visitors to the fake site were lulled into a sense of comfort. Unfortunately, people who entered orders on the fake site received no tickets but had their credit card numbers stolen.

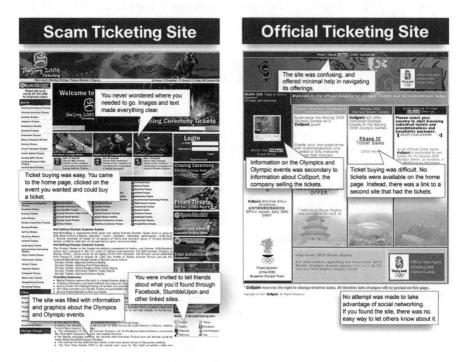

Figure 8-1   *Fake Sites Can Look Better Than the Real Thing*

Some malware is still distributed as email attachments, but the more successful of these campaigns also depend heavily on social engineering to make the emails appear trustworthy so that you'll open them. (And the more sophisticated malware payloads available today can avoid being filtered out by antimalware solutions for a longer period, also increasing the email-borne malware's chance of getting through.) Recent successful email-borne malware campaigns include

■   Emails with attachments pretending to be "shipping department profit and loss statement" spreadsheets, which are highly personalized and sent to specific company executives.

■   Emails with attachments that pretend to be delivery confirmation requests from major shipping services, such as UPS or FedEx.

■ Emails that are highly personalized and pretend to be from tax authorities or consumer information bureaus, asking company executives to fill out the attached form in response to a tax concern or business complaint.

The social engineering involved in the preceding attacks often is irresistible to end users. How many of us wouldn't open an email from FedEx saying the package we sent on a certain date couldn't be delivered, especially if we had sent off a few packages that same week?

Advanced social engineering techniques usually involve additional information to personalize the attack and make it seem closer to legitimate traffic. To support this next wave of personalized attacks, criminals mine social networking sites for personal information that they can later use to personalize phishing messages sent to you, or to your colleagues, friends, or family.

Spamming and Phishing Get Targeted

Spamming and phishing are becoming much more sophisticated. Spam emails use highly topical subject lines, often related to current news events. The content in the message looks and sounds much more legitimate and professional than it used to. Spam often closely mimics legitimate senders' messages—not just in style but by "spoofing" the sender information, making it look like it comes from a reputable sender.

The increasing personalization and sophistication of spam messages benefits the spammer in two ways:

■ If it looks more like legitimate traffic, modern spam is more likely to slip past anti-spam software.

■ Because of the targeted content, more people will actually open the message. More messages getting through filters and more messages opened means increased profits for the spammer.

The majority of spam is still classified as *mass mailing spam*, for example, billions of copies of messages for illegal pharmaceutical sites or the venerable get-rich-quick scams. The original mass mailers would send large volumes of the same message from a few source locations on the Internet. But these types of campaigns are relatively easy for spam filters to block through keyword analysis and blacklists of the mailing sources. Modern mass mailing spam still involves billions (yes, billions) of messages per attack, but they typically come from millions of different sources—coordinated by botnets—to obscure their origin. A modern mass mailer can also include tens of thousands of variations in the content, to defy keyword or signature filters.

Fighting Spam

Stopping today's mass mailers requires large data collection networks and sophisticated correlation techniques that can identify common elements or fingerprints in the campaign. Only a small number of antispam vendors have the reach required to sample enough of these huge attacks and the technical resources required to analyze them.

The constantly increasing investment required to keep a spam filter accurate has led to the consolidation of the spam filter industry. Five years ago, more than a hundred plausible vendors existed; today, you can count them on one hand.

In addition to the increasingly sophisticated camouflage techniques of the high-volume spammers, more and more spam campaigns are aimed at specific groups, such as sports fans, or at people in certain geographic regions. These campaigns are even harder to detect due to the low volume associated with a targeted attack. Figure 8-2 shows the increasing trend of targeted attacks over time.

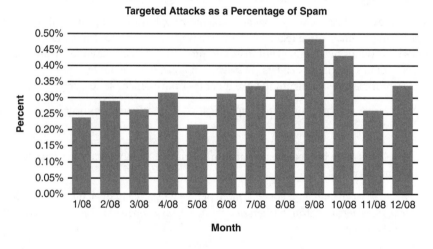

Figure 8-2   *Targeted Attacks as a Percentage of Overall Spam*

For phishing spam that's aimed at obtaining personal or financial information, targeted phishing—also known as *spear-phishing*—has become the norm. Figure 8-3 shows how spear-phishing has become more frequent, and more lucrative, than traditional spam campaigns.

Some recent spear-phishing campaigns involved personalized messages sent to customers of specific banks or frequent flyer programs to prompt them to log in or input their account information on a phishing website. Other campaigns are based on personalized emails sent to company executives, claiming they were subpoenaed or needed to give information to tax authorities. Figure 8-4 shows a sample targeted phishing email.

Criminals aren't solely depending on email and websites to practice their craft. Text messaging to mobile phones, combined with fake call-center setups, are another way they gather information. For instance, they send an SMS (Short Message Service, or text message) that claims to be from a regional bank to mobile phone numbers in a certain area code. The SMS asks recipients to call a number to confirm their account information, but of course, the number isn't actually that of the bank. It's staffed by criminals.

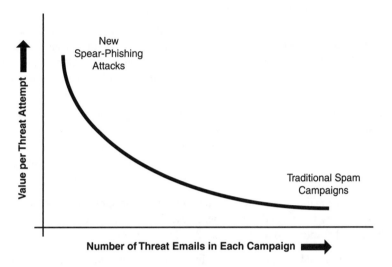

Figure 8-3 *Spear-Phishing Attacks Versus Traditional Spam*

Figure 8-4 *Example of a Targeted Phishing Email*

Mining Online Social Networks

Online criminals have also been tapping into all the information—and contacts—available on social networks such as Facebook and MySpace. They're hijacking accounts to beg for money, mining social networking sites for information for phone scams, and constantly finding new ways to capitalize on the wealth of information available on online social networks.

Take the case of Bryan Rutberg. As reported on MSNBC.com's Redtape Chronicles, his Facebook account was hijacked.[5] The online criminal reset the password to lock Rutberg out of his own account, after possibly having obtained the original using a clever phishing

continues

email. Then the criminals changed Rutberg's Facebook "status" message saying he was in trouble while on vacation overseas, and, claiming that his credit card wasn't working, that he needed a quick loan that he'd repay when he got back home.

This was a variant of a classic "419 scam"—named after the section of Nigeria's penal code that covers them because Nigeria is where both classic versions of the scam (faxes or emails asking for assistance in obtaining large amounts of money from overseas bank amounts) and modern versions often originate. It worked; one of Rutberg's concerned friends wired over money.

Similar scams are run on other online social networks and will increase as people spend more of their online time and attention there.

Profit Motive

Much of today's malware has one goal in common: financial profit. Hackers used to create viruses largely for fun and glory. These days, hackers and online criminals are part of a sophisticated shadow economy that wants to make money.

Like any maturing industry, the online crime market has begun to segment into specializations. Some online criminals focus on the social engineering, marketing, and fulfillment of merchandise. Others work on building and maintaining massive bot networks that they make available for rent. And some organizations specialize in building and deploying tools for malware creation and delivery.

Talented developers have been creating ever-better variants of malware. They create malware for a specific, popular purpose and sell it "as is" or together with tech support. They also develop custom malware for specific projects. Of the types of malware now for sale or rent, the following are just a few examples:

- Mass blog-posting tools

- Volume spamming tools

- Account-generating tools for webmail accounts or community posting sites, such as Craigslist

- Keylogging programs

- Botnet management tools

Because malware is generating significant profits for online criminals, they'll keep investing in it. That means more new kinds of malware that take advantage of weaknesses in both existing and newly popular technologies and tools, and malware that works even harder to be efficient and stay hidden.

But how exactly are online criminals profiting from malware? And who's reaping these financial returns? In the next chapter, we explore the business aspects of malware.

Endnotes

[1] Nichols, Shaun. "Ransomware attacks target Symbian mobiles," VNUnet. March 5, 2008. http://www.vnunet.com/vnunet/news/2211194/ransomware-goes-mobile.

[2] Provos, Niels. "All Your iFrame Are Point to Us," Google Online Security Blog. February 11, 2008. http://googleonlinesecurity.blogspot.com/2008/02/all-your-iframe-are-point-to-us.html.

[3] Weber, Tim. "Criminals 'may overwhelm the web,'" BBC News. January 25, 2007. http://news.bbc.co.uk/1/hi/business/6298641.stm.

[4] Cluley, Graham. "Hackers infect BusinessWeek website via SQL Injection attack," Graham Cluley's blog on Sophos.com. September 15, 2008. http://www.sophos.com/blogs/gc/g/2008/09/15/hackers-infect-businessweek-website-via-sql-injection-attack/.

[5] Sullivan, Bob. "Facebook ID Theft Targets 'Friends,'" MSNBC.com. January 30, 2009. http://redtape.msnbc.com/2009/01/post-1.html.

References

Cisco 2008 Annual Security Report. www.cisco.com/en/US/prod/collateral/vpndevc/securityreview12-2.pdf.

IronPort Targeted Phishing Overview PPT 061308—Nilesh Bhandari, IronPort.

IronPort Targeted Phishing Security Trends Overview. www.ironport.com/pdf/ironport_targeted_phishing.pdf.

IronPort 2008 Internet Malware Trends Report—Storm and the Future of Social Engineering. http://www.ironport.com/malwaretrends/.

Cisco IntelliShield Cyber Risk Reports. http://tools.cisco.com/security/center/cyberRiskReport.x.

ZDnet Zero Day blog. http://blogs.zdnet.com/security/.

CNet Security News. http://news.cnet.com/security/.

The Spamhaus Project news blog. http://www.spamhaus.org/newsindex.lasso.

Chapter 9

Who Are These Guys?

This chapter includes the following topics:

- The Business of Malware

- Studying Pharmaceutical Spam

- Other Links in the Global Chain

- Taking on the Bad Guys

So who are the online criminals who have made malware such a big business? How are they using malware, botnets, spam, and phishing attacks—and Web 2.0 tools and technologies—to profit?

They range from small-time crooks to highly sophisticated international organizations. These organizations offer botnets for rent; create and distribute malware; pay affiliates for spamming, marketing, and fulfillment services; and engage in a host of other bad behavior.

In this chapter, we take a look behind the curtain of the online criminal ecosystem— from malware developers to shadowy cybercrime networks that might have ties to governments.[1]

The Business of Malware

Many different types of online criminals profit from malware and are involved in its "shadow economy." This is a thriving ecosystem that in many ways parallels the legitimate Internet economy.

Many of the online criminals in this shadow economy are no longer the developers of modern malware. Nowadays, malware development is often an outsourced function, as are other elements of the chain, such as creating networks of "bots" or hijacked computers.

The online criminal economy is becoming highly specialized. Malware developers used to be thought of as the "fringe" element—people who couldn't get or hold down a job creating legitimate software. They were seen as antisocial hackers who cared more about fame than gainful employment. Or they were seen as part of a vast pool of "script kiddies"—young amateurs trying to gain fame by hacking into servers, networks, and websites but using malicious tools actually created by other, more skilled hackers higher up the totem pole.

Today, many of the authors and users of malware are a different breed. They're sophisticated, organized, and professional.

Talented software developers now use their skills to develop malware and sell or rent the results to online criminals. Malware developers are even offering "suites" of exploit software or annual support packages for sale or rent. The Rock Phish "phishing made easy" kit, MPack, WebAttacker, and NeoSploit are just some examples of professionally developed malware tools that have cropped up in the last few years.

The online criminals who use malware today do so to exploit weaknesses in online technologies and human nature. These criminals are a diverse bunch, ranging from organized criminal gangs to small-time crooks.

Distributed Denial of Service Attacks Using Botnets

DDoS attacks usually use a botnet to generate an overwhelming number of requests to view a website. Too many requests in too short a time overwhelm the web server, meaning that no one anywhere can access the site. And because these requests are coming from hundreds or thousands of different IP addresses (the different compromised computers in the botnet), they're much harder to block than an old-fashioned denial-of-service attack, where many server requests come from only a handful of IP addresses.

Sometimes, DDoS attacks are accidental. Several major banks have had their email interrupted for days because they were receiving bounce messages coming from thousands of legitimate mail gateways across the Internet. The bounce messages were a result of large fraudulent "phishing" emails that were sent out with the bank's domain as a return address. Because the majority of these spam messages bounce, the bank was an unwitting target of an email DDoS attack.

Small-time crooks might use popular social networking or Web 2.0 sites to find victims for their real-world scams. Online scam scenarios frequently used include a "friend" claiming to be in distress while traveling abroad, offers for fake rental houses, and fake housemate scams.

One criminal even posted a help-wanted ad on Craigslist.com to hire people to dress in a particular outfit and be at a specific location at a certain time. When they arrived, it became clear that the criminal used them as inadvertent look-alike decoys to mask his getaway from robbing an armored car.[2]

These types of criminal activities usually net each perpetrator just a couple hundred or thousand dollars—if the victims fall for them at all. Even the classic technique of starting or threatening a DDoS attack against an organization's servers or websites, and then blackmailing the organization into paying money to have the attack called off, is starting to feel rather limited in scope because there's more cash to be made in more sophisticated schemes.

The really big money is in large-scale operations. The biggest moneymakers appear to be criminal operations that use botnets to send out pharmaceutical spam and pump-and-dump stock investment spam. Another large-scale business is online fraud associated with phishing for people's personal and financial information. We take a closer look at pharmaceutical spam and how it can reap rewards for its perpetrators.

Studying Pharmaceutical Spam

Pharmaceutical spam is an amazing example of how lucrative and well organized some of these online criminal activities can be. Why is it such a big business? Consider the challenges faced by someone trying to save money on pharmaceuticals by traveling to Canada or Mexico, where costs are typically much lower than in the United States. Or consider the challenges faced by someone who has no insurance, yet needs expensive prescription drugs.

This is the eager market that the pharmaceutical fraudsters tapped into—that is, a ready audience of buyers who were eager to take a "too good to be true" deal at face value.

To find out more about the world of online drug sales, Patrick Peterson, a Cisco Fellow focusing on security, and his team spent significant time between 2006 and 2008 researching the back story behind today's pharmaceutical spam.[3] The team uncovered details about the inner workings of these "spam machines," and the technology used to drive these enterprises.

Modern high-volume spamming campaigns, including pharmaceutical spam, are sent out by botnets consisting of compromised computers, or botnet nodes, whose owners might never be aware that their PC is doing nefarious deeds. Each compromised computer can send out up to 40,000 spam emails per hour. So a network of tens of thousands can easily send billions of messages in short order. The nodes often host the websites to which these increasingly clever emails point.

In the particular attack studied by Peterson and his team, they found more than 1.5 billion messages coming from 100,000 different botnets spanning 119 countries. The spam attack had approximately 2000 different content permutations that changed every 12 minutes to evade traditional spam filters. The spam messages referenced more than 1500 unique web domains, which pointed to one of 12 different site designs.

The people behind the pharmaceutical spam use the botnet's architecture and obfuscation techniques to hide where the emails are coming from, and to hide and rapidly change which computers are hosting the websites. In this particular attack, they moved the hosting web servers every 15 minutes.

The criminals also hide who registered the domain names they use, and they make the websites that offer the pharmaceuticals—Viagra, Cialis, painkillers, and a host of other prescription drugs—look as credible and real as possible, as shown in Figure 9-1.

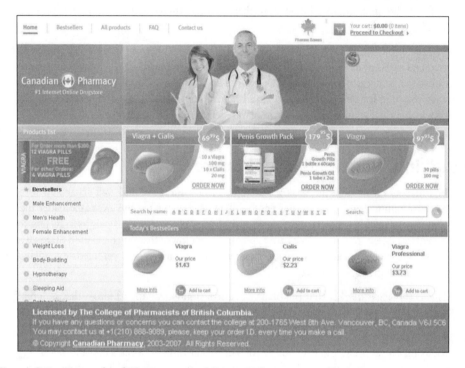

Figure 9-1 *Example of Pharmaceutical Spam Website*

The researchers noted that the then-home page for a company called MyCanadianPharmacy looked legitimate. The site included pictures of the corporate headquarters, a photo and biography of the site's founder, Dr. Jack Poppins, and claims of accreditation from the BBBOnLine Reliability Program, Canadian International Pharmacy Association, and PharmacyChecker.com.

According to the webpage, Dr. Poppins was an accomplished brain surgeon who was tired of the U.S. government's unwillingness to provide affordable medications to its citizens. So, he and a group of colleagues formed MyCanadianPharmacy to make affordable medication available to all. Dr. Poppins even invited customers to visit the headquarters in Toronto. The Cisco research team sent a group to the Toronto address, but all they found was a vacant lot next to a sandwich shop.

When they ordered samples from the various websites, they received pills that came in hand-addressed envelopes postmarked in different cities in India and China. Following up on the return addresses of these mailings, they found apartments in neighborhoods not far from pharmaceutical plants. According to analyses from an independent laboratory, the drugs received ranged from having no active ingredient, to the proper amount, to 50 percent more than the specified amount. None of the medications were manufactured by the proper patent holder.

One interesting note from the research was that the team promptly received an order confirmation, a request to rate the shopping experience, and the offer of a discount for future purchases. The organization behind it is clearly interested in making money by investing in positive customer service. The customer service contacts for the various websites all seemingly connected to MyCanadianPharmacy appeared to come from a single entity. "I'd never seen cybercrime like this. It's a professionally managed, huge business," says Peterson. There was even a working phone number where buyers could inquire about the status of their order.

For online criminals, the investment in creating the websites, the spam campaigns, renting or running the botnets, and renting or running a fulfillment operation is well worth it. With proper execution, these investments can deliver big returns.

The MyCanadianPharmacy websites alone have been estimated to generate sales of US $150 million per year. (The sites open and close under different domain names to stay a step ahead of regulators.) And that's just one out of thousands of similar sites run by online criminals.

Other Links in the Global Chain

Besides malware developers and the online criminals reaping the profits from fake or low-grade drugs, the online criminal ecosystem includes many more players. Tracking who and where these people are exactly is tricky, but information has come to light on several organizations.

The GlavMed (SpamIt) organization could be viewed as the "affiliate program" for pharmaceutical sales. For instance, the botnet owners send spam driving web traffic to GlavMed sites and GlavMed pays commissions to botnet owners for each pharmaceutical order. GlavMed takes the order, ships the product, and provides customer support enabling the botnet owner to focus on malware and spam.

GlavMed (SpamIt) might have connections to the Russian Business Network (RBN), a notorious cybercrime organization with possible ties to one or more Russian political figures. RBN has been associated with Internet hosting services for spammers, child-pornography rings, phishers and identity theft, creating and distributing malware, and all kinds of illegal online activities.

The Rock Phish gang is an online criminal network that offers phishing malware and runs botnets out of Romania and nearby countries.

New Zealand-based HerbalKing "spamvertised" dubious pharma-related products and ran campaigns for counterfeit luxury consumer goods through billions of emails sent by botnets. It was shut down in 2008 after a collaborative effort between the U.S. Federal Trade Commission, and law enforcement in New Zealand.

Two North American Internet service providers, Atrivo/InterCage and McColo, provided hosting services to notorious spammers and websites used to command and control botnets. They were both shut down in late 2008. (Industry researchers, media organizations, and law enforcement agencies worked together to make this happen.)

After each of the two shutdowns, the worldwide volume of spam dropped significantly for a while (see Figure 9-2). That is until the online criminals found alternative hosting solutions. "Right after the McColo shutdown, we saw a major drop in spam volume right away," said Nick Edwards, product line manager for the Cisco IronPort email security appliances. "But that kind of reprieve doesn't last. The Internet economy is so fluid that it's not hard to restart your business elsewhere in the world."

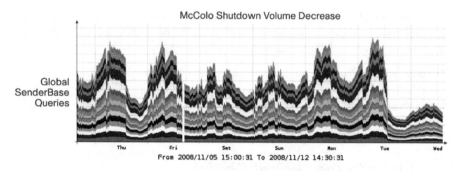

Figure 9-2   *Spam Volumes Drop After Shutdowns of Key Hosting Providers*

A crimeware server located in Argentina was found to contain more than 200,000 stolen login credentials, and a new version of Neosploit, a malware kit previously announced as dead by its creators (possibly to throw off industry watchdogs). According to Ian Amit, director of security research at Aladdin Knowledge Systems, who penetrated the server, as many as 250,000 PCs might have been successfully attacked when they visited websites that were compromised using Neosploit.[4]

Taking on the Bad Guys

Out on the Internet, many, many more online criminal organizations and activities exist than can be listed here.

And it's an ongoing arms race between the activities of online criminals and the efforts of security researchers and law enforcement.

The malware that makes the attacks possible is becoming more refined and sophisticated. Meanwhile, online criminals continue to get more specialized, and in many cases, more professional. And if the profits remain big, for every online criminal or gang that's stopped, ten replacements will be ready and waiting in the wings.

But that doesn't mean we should just throw up our hands in despair.

Researchers and law enforcement collaborate more frequently on online criminal cases. And it's not just malware that's been getting better. Technological developments in several areas make it possible to effectively filter out and remove attacks by these criminals. The next chapter provides a closer look at some of the more promising technical solutions.

Endnotes

[1] Warren, Peter. "Hunt for Russia's Web Criminals." The Guardian. November 15, 2007. http://www.guardian.co.uk/technology/2007/nov/15/news.crime.

[2] "'Inner tube robber' charged in federal court." King5.com. November 26, 2008. http://www.komonews.com/news/local/35134614.html.

[3] Murphy Barrett, Victoria. "Spam Hunter." Forbes. July 23, 2007. http://www.forbes.com/forbes/2007/0723/054.html.

[4] Keizer, Gregg. "Hackers resurrect notorious attack tool kit." Computerworld. September 25, 2008. http://www.computerworld.com/action/article.do?command=viewArticleBasic& taxonomyName=Security&articleId=9115599.

References

Cisco 2008 Annual Security Report. www.cisco.com/en/US/prod/collateral/vpndevc/securityreview12-2.pdf.

IronPort 2008 Internet Malware Trends Report:-Storm and the Future of Social Engineering. http://www.ironport.com/malwaretrends/.

IronPort "Eye of the Storm" presentation, May 2008.

OECD 2008 Ministerial Background Report "Malicious Software (malware): A Security Threat to the Internet Economy." http://www.oecd.org/LongAbstract/ 0,3425,en_2649_33703_40724458_119666_1_1_1,00.html.

Cisco IntelliShield Cyber Risk Reports. http://tools.cisco.com/security/center/cyberRiskReport.x.

ZDnet Zero Day blog. http://blogs.zdnet.com/security/.

CNet Security News. http://news.cnet.com/security/.

The Spamhaus Project news blog. http://www.spamhaus.org/newsindex.lasso.

Chapter 10

Signs of Hope

This chapter includes the following topics:

- Harnessing the Network

- Scanning for Signatures

- Behavioral Analysis of Bad Code

- The Power of Reputation

- Global Threat Correlation

- Combining Countermeasures

The arms race between malware creators and security vendors isn't about to let up. Because there is profit to be made, malware will keep getting smarter, faster, and more dangerous. However, as you will read in this chapter, there is reason to believe that the security industry can combat threatening malware attacks and keep the Internet a generally (if not completely) safe place.

But delivering a "generally safe" Internet experience means IT professionals need to stay current on the latest technologies, and vendors must constantly reinvent themselves. For example, blacklists are considered a staple of traditional security. But these static systems can't keep up with real-time threats, or those from compromised but legitimate websites previously whitelisted.

Modern spam and malware campaigns have become much more targeted and randomized. Just a few years ago, spam and viruses resembled torrential floods—massive quantities of the same attack blasting across the Internet. Although the sheer volume of these pestilences caused disruption, it was relatively easy to identify and stop the outbreaks because they all looked the same.

Today, modern spam and malware resemble snowflakes in a snowstorm: Billions of individual snowflakes cloud the skies, but no two of them look exactly alike. This means they're much harder to block because they defy traditional signature systems.

Fortunately, for all the innovation in the malware industry, there are also significant amounts of innovation in threat defense. To stay abreast of sophisticated malware and spam campaigns, security vendors use antimalware technologies and techniques that harness the power of the network and take advantage of the dramatic processing power of multicore processors.

These techniques include

■ Signature-based malware scanning using multiple engines

■ Behavioral analysis of software to see if it engages in suspicious actions

■ Real-time reputation-based assessment and blocking of websites, URLs, and IP addresses

No single defense can beat the cunning of modern malware, yet a well-designed combination of different resources and techniques can provide the robust coverage organizations need for protection from today's most harmful attacks.

Harnessing the Network

Online criminals are making good use of the advantages offered by the Internet and today's high level of connectivity. Botnets, for instance, use the power of distributed networks. They control massive arrays of compromised computers all over the world and force them to perform malicious tasks. The results are far more damaging than would be possible with only a few computers in one location. As shown in Chapter 9, "Who Are These Guys?," modern botnets take advantage of cutting-edge peer-to-peer technology such as distributed hash tables to fan out to millions of nodes—with no single "head" that can be easily disabled. This lets botnet owners hide crucial elements of what they're doing in the cloud. It offers redundancy and scale. And it makes it hard to take them down.

Bad Guys Team Up

Meanwhile, today's malware is being composed to use multiple technologies and protocols, such as an email component and web components, for maximum effect and easy distribution. Email and web attacks are like Bonnie and Clyde: They work together to commit crimes online.

And it's not just the technology that works together. Modern malware attacks no longer come from a single entity. They are typically the product of a malware industry involving groups with different specializations—technology, botnet operations, marketing, and sourcing, to name a few. The collaborative nature of the modern online criminal ecosystem has become, ironically, a great example of the virtualized, distributed workforce. Online criminals are effectively using the Internet to conduct their business together. They are even paying each other through online payment services such as WebMoney or "gift" credit cards bought online.

But as online criminal activity advances, IT security needs to keep pace. To date, much security thinking has been based around "point" protection and solutions: Using different software solutions and hardware boxes on-site within the corporate network to scan and protect corporate data being accessed mostly from within an organization's office buildings. The systems are predominantly reactive, blocking a threat when it is clearly known to exist. With today's networked, constantly changing attacks, hardware boxes that don't talk to each other just can't keep up.

Staying in Front of the Threats

The past 100 years have shown us that free markets and the profit motive will find a way to overcome almost any obstacle. Although that generally means forward progress, in the case of malware, the innovation deployed in the name of illicit profits is remarkable. To counter this steady rise of sophisticated threats, leading security solutions must move beyond the traditional signature-based antivirus and IP-based blacklists.

Modern security needs to take advantage of the power of the network and the cloud just as much as today's productivity applications—and online criminals—do. This means:

- Creating a global shared security intelligence system to increase the speed and accuracy with which attacks are detected and responses are created.

- Finding new parameters to analyze in a particular piece of content—whether it's the construction of the webpage or email, or an assessment of the way a particular piece of code will behave.

- Looking beyond the contents of dataflow and considering the historical behavior of the server or entity originating the content.

These diverse security techniques must be *combined* onto a few efficient, integrated platforms, instead of stacking up many different security solution boxes that must each wheeze their way through checking all network traffic. Modern security systems need to deliver multilayer and often multivendor security scanning in a single integrated platform. This is not technically out of reach, and the approach yields much better protection with lower operational costs.

Scanning for Signatures

Scanning for signatures, the unique bits of code that can uniquely identify malicious software, is a time-tested technique for identifying malware. These threat-detection systems examine code for known patterns of "bad behavior" and compare this code to previously identified virus signatures.

However, signature scanning can be CPU-intensive. For this reason, most companies deploy multilayer scanning for latency-tolerant traffic, such as email (typically on the perimeter, the message store, and the endpoint). On the other hand, for real-time protocols such as web, IM (instant messaging), and VoIP (Voice over IP) traffic, the concerns over latency have kept most companies from deploying anything other than endpoint protection.

Most customers have recognized that a multilayer, multivendor approach to signature scanning is most effective. Although all major signature vendors appear to catch roughly the same amount of malware in the steady state, response times vary widely depending on the nature of the attack. Therefore, combining multiple vendors offers the most consistent coverage. An excellent source for comparing signature response times from different vendors is the not-for-profit avtests.org. Typical response times of signature vendors vary from less than 2 hours after a threat is discovered, to more than 24 to 36 hours for more complex threats.

Another aspect of multilayer scanning is that specialized vendors have created signature engines that look for certain classes of attack. A good example of this is Webroot, an antimalware company, which has extensive understanding of spyware and similar web-based malicious programs that are covert in nature. Webroot can do this by creating signatures that focus on contextual behavior of the program, instead of detecting static mal-code patterns employed by legacy vendors.

Advances in processing power driven by multicore processors have made it possible to vastly increase scanning speed and efficiency. Multiple processors running in parallel can now run multiple malware scanning engines from different vendors side by side, offering a higher catch rate with no perceptible latency.

Signature-based scanning is fundamental to a modern security solution. Signatures will always play an important role in defending networks in the future. However, it is widely recognized that signature scanning alone is not enough to stay in front of today's rapidly changing, more targeted attacks, and that the multilayer, multivendor approach is more effective.

Behavioral Analysis of Bad Code

Another technique used as a defense against malware is behavioral analysis of software. Where signature-based antimalware engines look at the bits that make up a piece of software, and compare those unique variances to code they've identified as malware, behavioral analysis monitors the *actions* a piece of software takes or intends to take.

For example, the analysis tries to identify suspicious behaviors, such as, "Why would a normal application need to overwrite these registries in Windows?" Or "Why is this software trying to create a buffer overflow that will give it root access?"

When the behavioral analysis determines that the action is something only malware is likely to do, it flags or blocks the suspect software, thus protecting the network.

Some behavioral systems attempt to analyze the code and predict its behavior if it were allowed to run. Other systems monitor the code when running on a client. Another variant is to shunt suspect traffic off to a "sandboxed" system (which is isolated from the rest of the network) and let it run under observation before it hits a real client.

However, all these approaches have limitations. Working on their own, they might not detect the most sophisticated threats. The challenge with behavioral systems is that they have false positives and often have extremely high latency or other performance issues. Behavioral analysis systems are a little bit like hydrogen fuel cells. The promise is strong, and as the technology advances it's highly likely they will become a widely used part of the security cocktail. But for most applications, they are too heavy, slow, and costly to realistically deploy. (At least they don't occasionally catch fire, as fuel cells sometimes do.)

For this reason, behavior-based systems have not been widely accepted in the market, and most companies rely on multiple layers of antivirus for email. However, for web traffic, most rely on only a single layer of antivirus technology at the endpoint. As many of us have experienced firsthand, despite these commonly deployed defenses, infections still occur all too often.

As previously stated, robust threat detection systems need to go beyond simple behavioral scanning if they are to be effective. This is where the multilayer and multivendor approach comes into play. When you have several solutions working together to block threats, for instance, signature scanning, web reputation filters, and pattern-based assessment techniques, the capability to block threats is greatly improved.

The Power of Reputation

Analyzing content either with signatures or behavioral techniques is an important part of the security mix. However, you can modify and randomize content in so many ways that content analysis alone will never yield a complete solution. Rather than examining the "what" that is being transmitted, a reputation system examines the "who" that is sending.

Assigning a reputation to Internet entities based on their current and past activities, and blocking or allowing traffic from them based on their real-time reputation, is a powerful technique for keeping malware at bay. It was pioneered by Cisco IronPort Systems in its email and web-filtering solutions several years ago and has now spread to the wider security community.[1]

This method relies on data gathered from the network to examine and assess the behavior of an Internet entity, such as a web object, a domain name, or an IP address of a server or computer on the Internet. Based on this analysis, a reputation score is assigned. Reputation needs to be a dynamic score, updated in as close to real time as possible to reflect any change in activities, such as a sudden spike in traffic associated with the server in question.

Essentially, reputation scoring works like personal credit scoring. Credit agencies monitor many factors, such as whether you've been paying bills on time, whether you suddenly made several big purchases, or whether you're applying for too many cards and loans at one time. If they think your behavior is off, your credit score, and correspondingly your ability to buy or borrow, immediately changes. Reputation scoring works in a similar fashion: The solution analyzes the available transaction data and creates a detailed score, which helps administrators set different security policies for different scoring ranges.

Looking at the real-time reputation of entities on the Internet is an extremely powerful tool in the fight to protect networks and users from online criminals. We've seen that modern attackers can instantly and constantly change the nature of the content of their attacks. But they cannot easily change their historical behavior or their reputation on the Internet.

Even a lack of history or a neutral reputation is still valuable information. It tells the security system, "We've never seen you before so we won't block you, but you can't have unlimited access." The incoming content can be limited (that is, don't accept executables from an unknown source), and the full battery of content inspection techniques can be applied, such as the multiple layers of signatures and behavioral analysis previously described. Reputation can be the basis to decide when to crack encrypted SSL sessions, and also apply limits about incoming content type and the data rate. Feeding the results of this inspection back into the central shared database helps to rapidly update either a positive or negative reputation.

Returning to the credit analogy, consider handling an application from a recent college graduate. The total lack of history doesn't mean the entity isn't worthy of credit or trust, but it does mean there should be careful limits. If the new entity attempts to buy a laptop computer with the credit, that transaction should be allowed. If the new entity attempts to buy a Ferrari with the new credit, that transaction should be blocked.

A critical difference between a reputation system and a traditional blacklist (see sidebar, "Much More than Blacklists") is that a blacklist is a list of known bad offenders. As such, most blacklists cover only a tiny portion of the active servers on the Internet.

A true reputation system, however, has something to say about every active server on the Internet. Measuring a sender's reputation requires having detailed knowledge of his behavior on the Internet over time. Accurately measuring the behavior of low-volume servers, such as those used in targeted attacks, requires an extremely large sample size across the entire Internet.

It's a classic signal processing problem. The big "mass mailer" viruses of early 2000 had volumes large enough to make it fairly easy to distinguish the outbreak from normal traffic. But as attacks become smaller and more targeted, the signal-to-noise-ratio drops, and a larger sample size is required to distinguish the signal (the attack) from the noise (the masses of normal Internet traffic).

When Cisco IronPort first invented this concept, the company developed a "threat telemetry" stream that allowed receiving mail systems to send traffic statistics back to a central database—in IronPort's case, the system was called SenderBase (now called Cisco SensorBase). As more and more IronPort appliances were deployed, the sample of Internet traffic grew and grew. Today, Cisco IronPort appliances protect eight of the ten largest ISPs in the world, and more than 25,000 of the world's largest institutions and enterprises.

As a result, SensorBase samples more than 35 percent of the world's email traffic. This data footprint enables IronPort to block more than 90 percent of incoming spam simply by analyzing the reputation of the sender.

This technique has proven to be remarkably robust over time. As spammers have migrated from text spam to image spam to PDF spam and now to email and web spam, the new attacks might fool a content-based filter, but the reputation of the sending server—mostly botnets—is still a huge "tell" that enables the IronPort filters to remain highly effective over time. Reputation also has the advantage of being CPU-efficient. The reputation score is precalculated in the cloud, so all that the receiving appliances need to execute the command is a simple lookup.

Reputation filtering is typically 10 or 20 times more CPU-efficient than signature-based scanning. As stated previously, signature-based scanning is a key part of a modern security solution, but it can't completely protect organizations from newer, more sophisticated attacks. This makes reputation a powerful first line of defense. If a state-of-the-art reputation system can eliminate 90 percent or more of the incoming traffic, it now becomes reasonable to run multiple arrays of antimalware signatures, or to run computationally intensive behavioral analysis on the remaining 10 percent of incoming traffic. Working together, a great reputation system and advanced content analysis will yield the cutting edge of protection.

Much More than Blacklists For a long time, online security systems have used identity as the basis of filtering. This technique revolved around the construct of a "blacklist."

A variety of not-for-profit antispam and antimalware organizations would detect a large amount of spam or malware or other illicit traffic coming from certain domains or IP addresses and add those to a blacklist. This list was then published freely to the community and used widely in early spam or web filters.

However, several big drawbacks to a blacklist exist. First, a blacklist is binary—either a sender is entirely guilty and should be fully blocked, or entirely innocent and should be given unlimited access. This is similar to driving a car with either full acceleration or full brakes applied. It makes for a pretty rough ride.

In today's world, rapidly evolving threats require a more sophisticated response. Having the capability to throttle a new sender and apply the highest levels of content inspection, and then tying the results of that inspection back into the reputation system in real time, creates a much more intelligent and robust response to new threats.

The second issue is coverage. A blacklist is a list of known offenders. As such, it typically covers only 10 to 20 percent of the active IP addresses on the Internet. A reputation system covers effectively 100 percent of the IP addresses on the Internet. A blacklist is similar to the list of bad check-passers sometimes seen on the cash register at a corner store. Unfortunately, anyone who passed a bad check at the store is not likely to come back.

A reputation system is more like a modern credit system, as previously discussed. All customers that come into the store swipe their cards, prompting a lookup on a database to get a credit score. The system then looks at the transaction, and if it is appropriate, signals the merchant to proceed. Like the sign on the cash register in the store, blacklists are still in use, but the threats have long since grown beyond a blacklist's capability to stop them.

Global Threat Correlation

As threats have evolved to become multiprotocol, using email and web together, reputation systems need to evolve to consider multiple traffic types as well. An excellent example of this is the interconnection between email and web security. On average, about 80 to 90 percent of spam contains a URL because it is a call to action to sell something. By analyzing the reputation of the referenced web server and the reputation of the sending email server, a more accurate decision can be made.

If a modern reputation system has access to web traffic on the scale of the email reputation system previously described, email and web behavior can be analyzed separately, and the results can be correlated. As shown in Chapter 9, botnets are used as multifunction attack platforms. One minute they're sending spam, the next minute they're hosting malware. Then, they might be launching a directed attack on a legitimate web server. By correlating these different traffic types in the cloud, a more comprehensive defense can be deployed.

If a web security appliance detects malware coming from a new site, that information is fed back to the central database. A few minutes later, if an IPS system in another part of the globe detects a suspicious flow from that same server, it's highly likely that this is a directed attack coming from a bot.

Expanding reputation from simply email to all network traffic types, and performing global correlation of threats against this database, provides the broadest, most comprehensive protection. Early results of this technique are impressive. For example, Cisco IPS systems that use global threat correlation have been found to yield a 300 percent increase in catch rate, while at the same time lowering false positives.

To make global threat correlation work, the central database needs to be extremely large. The system must have some knowledge of every publically routable IP address, even if the only information is that the IP is brand new and has just become active. This is still useful information: It conveys to the security appliances that this IP has no history and should not be given unlimited access. Volume and content restrictions should be applied and maximum signature or other analysis techniques should be engaged.

Global threat correlation also has some privacy implications. Every appliance participating in the network sends summary information back to the central database. These issues are mitigated by having robust and mature processes in place to safeguard any data collected. Furthermore, the data collected is always composed of just summary statistics, not the actual network traffic. So there is no way for sensitive information, such as personal data, earnings, or financial information, to find its way into the telemetry stream.

One of the most important reasons why this approach succeeds is the alignment of incentives. A modern security system can't catch what it can't see. As a result, turning on the telemetry usually has a profound impact on performance in the customer's network. Thus, customers are motivated to turn on data sharing to protect their own users and for the good of the Internet.

According to a tech consultant for a leading advertising and marketing agency in the United Kingdom, "Web reputation technology[2] allows the agency to protect its users, but still allows them to get their jobs done seamlessly." The agency uses web reputation technology to block 19,000 web elements a day, but it still can give its employees access to sites they need to collaborate and to work more productively.

Combining Countermeasures

Although no perfect defense against online threats exists, insight can provide the "good guys" with a significant advantage over online criminals who work harder to stealth their attacks by making them more targeted and cross-protocol.

This is the thinking behind the Cisco Global Threat Correlation initiative, which is helping to build a "satellite view" of the Internet so that anomalies and potential attacks across different types of traffic and protocols can be identified early. (Cisco is in a unique position to deliver next-generation Internet security. Cisco products touch almost every packet sent over the Internet at some point, and more than 30 percent of the world's email is received and processed by Cisco appliances.)

Using telemetry from the millions of Cisco devices in service worldwide, Cisco Security Intelligence Operations (SIO) examines traffic patterns looking for anomalies. The traffic patterns come from all types of organizations, including major ISPs, companies ranging from the Fortune 50 to tens of thousands of small businesses, and an array of universities. This geographic and demographic diversity provides Cisco with a broad sample of global Internet traffic patterns. Cisco SIO is staffed by hundreds of researchers operating in five locations worldwide, processing terabytes of data about Internet traffic patterns every day.

This level of analysis and insight will be increasingly critical for Internet security moving forward. To stay ahead of Internet attacks, security organizations will need to use a multilayered "cocktail" approach: looking at different protocols and combining best-of-breed technology from different vendors in an integrated fashion. They must harness the power of the network, as today's mobile workforce—and the online criminals preying on them—already do.

Leading security vendors can offer customers best-of-breed performance with multilayer defense by embedding technology from multiple vendors into a single, integrated product. (This is an approach Cisco has adopted with all its relevant security products, offering customers a choice of multiple signature vendors tightly integrated into a single, high-performance chassis.) But cooperation between security vendors goes beyond OEM agreements to embed signatures. Most major players in the industry enter into formal or informal data-sharing agreements. Cisco, for example, has data-sharing agreements in place with more than 150 entities—ISPs, nonprofits, and other security companies.

Insight. Cooperation. Collaboration. These are the signs of hope that send a clear signal to the online criminal economy that although their methods of attack might be smarter, faster, and more dangerous, so too are the defenses designed to deflect them.

Endnotes

[1] Keong, Lee Min. "Symantec to identify safe software by 'reputation,'" ZDnet. October 24, 2008. http://news.zdnet.com/2100-9595_22-243676.html.

[2] Reference to IronPort's Web Reputation technology.

Reference

Cisco 2008 Annual Security Report.
http://www.cisco.com/en/US/prod/collateral/vpndevc/securityreview12-2.pdf.

Chapter 11

Acceptable Use Policies

This chapter includes the following topics:

- The Inevitable Evolution of AUPs

- Gen X/Gen Y "Problem"

- "Necessary" Noncompliance

- AUPs Versus the Will of the Employees

The rapid consumerization of IT and the growing popularity of mobile devices and interactive Web 2.0 applications are forcing companies to move away from their technological comfort zone and traditional notions of how their employees should go about the business of doing work. And as the line between personal and work computing continues to dissolve, management and IT leadership struggle to create realistic acceptable use policies (AUP) that apply in the Web 2.0 world.

Today's organizations face a formidable challenge: developing progressive but flexible AUPs that also preserve data and network security. Companies also need tools that provide the organization with an appropriate level of control over how employees use and interact with consumer technologies, but don't interfere with their productivity or job satisfaction.

The Inevitable Evolution of AUPs

AUPs outline the rules of behavior that employees are expected to follow when using company resources—for example, not using a business email account for personal use, not viewing sexually explicit websites via the company's Internet connection, or not accessing online shopping, trading, or entertainment sites during working hours.

Most companies already have some type of AUP, but many find their "laws on the books" don't translate well to the Web 2.0 work environment. They're often so restrictive that they're impossible to enforce. They stifle creativity and collaboration. They hinder workflow. And they make employees unhappy.

In the mid-1990s, when Internet use in business and on the home front was not yet widespread, companies drafted AUPs with strict guidelines for their employees. Accessing the Internet and using email for personal reasons during work hours was forbidden. These reactionary and less-than-insightful policies not only were unpopular with employees, but also impossible to enforce.

Human nature and curiosity would quickly prove to be too powerful to contain the Internet. Keep in mind that for most consumers in the 1990s, the workplace was the only place to get access to the Internet. And for years, it remained the most convenient place to find a fast connection.

Not surprisingly, people took full advantage of this "free" access and happily spent many of their work hours covertly learning how to send email, buy things, play games, and do whatever else they considered fun and interesting in this new place called "online." And most did so regardless of any policy their employer mandated.

Gen X/Gen Y "Problem"

Although employees might have been much less overt about such activities in the past, today they unabashedly use workplace technology for personal reasons. In the first few years of their professional life, many Generation Xers witnessed the Internet's arrival and subsequent, near-overnight transformation of the "20th century office" into the "21st century work environment."

No strangers to using personal computers for work and play, Gen Xers were quick to fully embrace Internet use both professionally and personally. In response, many employers created AUPs simply to keep their workers from being too distracted by the pleasures of the Web while on the job.

Although employers might have been able to temporarily contain the online habits of their Gen X employees, Generation Y—or "Millennials"—have been a different story. Most Millennials have known only a "wired world" their entire life. And they don't understand or accept the concept of compartmentalizing their technology use. They expect to be always connected—at home, on the job, and everywhere in between.

A highly restrictive AUP literally puts locks and chains on the primary tools Millennials use for communication and expression in the workplace *and* in their personal life. (For example, Gen Y workers are passionate about Web 2.0 applications, such as social networking and instant messaging. In fact, for many Millennials, social networks have completely replaced traditional email.)

Russell Graham, network services manager at Wesley College in Melbourne, Australia, knows very well how hard it is to contain the Internet habits of Gen Y. The private school, which has approximately 3,200 students, gives notebook computers to all students in fifth grade and above. The students are required to sign an AUP that provides guidelines for email and Internet use, including a stipulation that their laptops not be used to access "blocked or inappropriate" sites, according to Graham.

Wesley College currently does not permit students to access popular social networking sites such as Facebook. Graham says this is to avoid exposure to malware and other threats, and to keep students from viewing inappropriate content online. (The school does allow students to visit YouTube.)

However, the policy does not prevent students from trying their very best to get around the rules and access forbidden sites. And according to Graham, they are rather good at it.

"I'd say our biggest problem with students is anonymous proxies, which they use to try to access sites such as Facebook," says Graham. "As soon as an anonymous proxy is working, it spreads throughout the student body very quickly, and then all our policies go out the window. Anonymous proxies are created every day. You just can't keep up with it."

No doubt, as more Millennials enter the workforce in the years ahead, highly restrictive AUPs that do not acknowledge the obvious lack of separation between personal and business use of technology are going to be impossible to enforce. Consider the global trends highlighted in the 2008 survey by Cisco and U.S.-based market research firm, Insight Express, "The Challenge of Data Leakage for Businesses and Employees Around the World":

■   Nearly 80 percent of workers who use a company-issued computer for personal matters send or receive email through a personal email account regularly.

■   Most workers who use their company-issued desktop or notebook computer for personal matters do so every day.

■   Approximately 50 percent of employees use their work computer for personal research and online banking.

■   More than half of workers who have changed the security settings on their company-issued laptop to view restricted websites did so because they wanted to visit them, regardless of company policy, as shown in Figure 11-1.

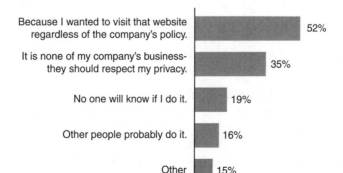

Figure 11-1   *Reasons for Altering Security Settings*

"Necessary" Noncompliance

A second set of findings from the same Cisco study revealed that most businesses have security policies and acceptable use guidelines in place today—yet employees often defy or ignore them. What prompts their noncompliance? Two things: Employees don't know the policies exist, or they have to circumvent rules in order to do their jobs well.

According to the report "Data Leakage Worldwide: The Effectiveness of Security Policies," which was based on the Cisco global data leakage study, "Fifty-six percent of IT professionals report that security policies are communicated to new hires during orientation, yet only 32 percent of employees say they were educated. This statistic reveals a significant disconnect between the beliefs of IT professionals and newly hired employees regarding the communication of security policies."[1] (See Figure 11-2.)

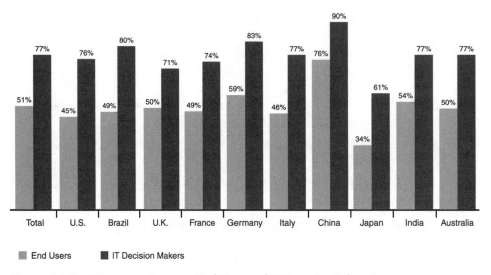

Figure 11-2   *Disconnect Between End User and IT Security Policy Awareness*

It should be noted that many companies leave discussions about policies, including acceptable use, not to their IT departments, but their human resources staff, who perfunctorily inform—and, in all fairness, are not in a position to truly educate—employees about these types of security policies upon hiring.

One of the global data leakage study's most significant findings is that although IT believes employees are noncompliant with policies for various reasons—including apathy—42 percent of workers surveyed worldwide said the top factor prompting their noncompliance is that policies are not in alignment with the reality of the tools they need to accomplish their jobs. In short, they feel compelled to break the rules set by their employer to do their work.

In addition, nearly half of workers surveyed worldwide said they felt their company's security policy was out of date, and the majority complained of corporate policies being too rigid and unfair. As the Cisco global study on data leakage revealed, a significant population of today's workers feel constricted, instead of enabled and empowered, by the technology their employers want them to use.

Many businesses today rely on systems, devices, and applications that simply cannot support today's fast-evolving Web 2.0 work environment. Once upon a time, the workplace was where to find cutting-edge technology, but it's fair to say that at many organizations today, *legacy* is the word. And in the interest of getting business done more efficiently, employees literally feel forced to create their own workstations and business processes.

They assemble the products and applications they feel best meet their work *and* personal needs, and are demanding that their employer support their choices. Because they *are* getting their work done more efficiently, they think nothing of whether they might be violating their company's AUP. That is, until their activities are "exposed" somehow by active enforcement or deployment of a policy that restricts use of Web 2.0 technology and unsupported devices.

A technology consultant who specializes in the advertising/media industry says that when a U.K.-based agency he consults for decided, in the interest of regulatory compliance demands and data security, to block employee use of online collaboration tools such as Google Docs, it created an uproar.

The change in policy revealed that several teams at the agency were using these applications to collaborate every day with each other and with clients. According to the consultant, one creative team was so far along with their work on one project that IT had to allow them to continue using Google Docs because there was simply no other way to finish the assignment on time. (He adds that use of Google Docs in that particular case was actually prompted by the client.)

Beyond seeing that one project through to completion, however, the agency intends to maintain its strict policy about use of Web 2.0 applications by employees—at least, for now.

"The agency has been getting loads of grief about blocking these types of applications," says the consultant. "People want to collaborate. But it's not that the agency wants to stop the collaboration. It's because they have no control over it. For example, if someone leaves the organization, who is in charge of getting rid of their password to log on? If the agency allowed use of Google Docs, that employee could spend their time before leaving taking all the documents. To be fair, the employee can still do it in other ways, but it's harder."

AUPs Versus the Will of the Employees

One other factor helping to blur any dividing line between use of technology for personal and business reasons is the remote working trend. Remote working has become a common business practice at many companies, instead of just a privilege for a chosen few.

Businesses have greatly loosened the reins on remote working, particularly over the past five years, due to advances in mobile technology, the demands of the global economy, and pressure from employees for greater work/life balance. Allowing employees to work from home regularly helps organizations maintain a 24/7 workforce. It took no time at all for people to become accustomed to using their own equipment at home for business purposes, and for the company-issued laptop to transform into the modern-day briefcase.

The powerful forces changing today's workforce have many companies realizing that while they might be able to put the clamps on certain practices, ultimately, they cannot stop the pace of technology. Nor can they control the will of their workers. And the question is, should they keep trying? After all, prohibiting use of Web 2.0 tools and applications can hurt the organization by stifling innovation, preventing greater productivity, and creating a work environment where employees think they're treated unfairly.

Some companies are also recognizing that allowing their workers to purchase and use their own devices in the workplace can be cost-effective for the organization in the long term, by absolving the employer of the responsibility of equipping their workforce with every item of technology necessary. And with more organizations warming to cloud computing and SaaS (Software as a Service), and the concept of virtualization, there is even less reason to mandate that employees access critical business applications only through company-issued devices.

Most organizations are still far away from embracing a culture of "openness" where technology use is concerned, but employee demand—and better technology—ultimately will change that. Right now, though, for many companies it's a matter of accepting one new device or application at a time.

"The exchange server that belongs to the agency I consult for doesn't support iPhones at the moment, but they have so many requests from employees who want to use them that I expect they'll probably end up making a policy that supports their use," says the U.K.-based tech consultant. "It will probably be: iPhone or BlackBerry, you decide."

He adds, however, that for the foreseeable future, the agency will continue to support only company-issued devices. "Employees are coming to the agency's IT department all the time and saying, 'I've got my own BlackBerry. Can't I put it on the BlackBerry Enterprise Server?' But they don't allow that."

The flood of new devices and applications moving into the enterprise from the consumer space is accentuating the need to revamp the corporate AUP. However, determining what makes a relevant, repeatable, and enforceable policy employees are likely to follow isn't easy.

It's not only because today's AUPs are more complicated. It's also because IT must take a more active role in enforcing policies, adapting them when necessary, and assessing risk to the organization related to the use of certain technologies. As Cisco vice president, IT-Global Client Services and Operations Rami Mazid explains, "Security policies, including AUPs, should never be a onetime event. They must be flexible and reviewed regularly."

Employee education is also important. As the Cisco 2008 global study on data leakage revealed, employee education about IT security and policy is an area in need of improvement at most organizations. Some of the more progressive AUPs enforced today at leading companies are not just focused on improving data and network security, but also potential legal quagmires for the organization, such as inflammatory content and sexual harassment claims due to employees misbehaving intentionally, or simply making bad decisions, while online.

AUPs have been, historically, "black and white" mandates: You can't go to this site, and you can't go to that site. Now, Web 2.0 is creating a gray area. AUPs are becoming more about what your online persona can and cannot do. It dictates what tools and applications you can and cannot use for work, even if they help you do your job better.

It's true that companies are facing real liabilities around how their employees use the Internet—from file sharing to posting videos to blogging to trading jokes on a social networking site. But the reality is, you can't just shut these things off. And sticking your head in the sand is not an option.

Web 2.0 must be faced, and for many sound business reasons, embraced. Organizations need more nimble AUPs that enable employees to use devices and applications that provide a combination of personal and business value. This has profound implications for the tools currently available to support AUPs. The network architecture and the gateway processing systems need to change to enable enterprises to safely embrace mobility and Web 2.0.

This does make AUPs more complicated. But allowing employees to shop online and look at videos on YouTube while on the job is a good thing for the company. Seriously. As more corporations turn to social media for marketing or for better communications with customers, the wave cannot be stopped. We have entered a world where business and personal computing are, inextricably, one.

Endnote

[1] Data Leakage Worldwide: The Effectiveness of Security Policies.
http://www.cisco.com/en/US/solutions/collateral/ns170/ns896/ns895/white_paper_c11-503131.html.

References

"The Challenge of Data Leakage for Businesses and Employees Around the World."
http://www.cisco.com/en/US/solutions/collateral/ns170/ns896/ns895/Cisco_STL_Data_Leakage_2008_PR1.pdf.

Cisco 2008 Annual Security Report.
www.cisco.com/en/US/prod/collateral/vpndevc/securityreview12-2.pdf.

Nicolett, Mark and Pescatore, John. "Optimal Security Approaches for the Secure Use of Consumer IT," Gartner Research, April 22, 2008.

Chapter 12

The Realities of
Data Loss

This chapter includes the following topics:

- One Breach, Multiple Shockwaves

- Insiders

- Compliance Pitfall

- DLP: Chasing Rainbows?

Most security organizations devote the majority of their time, attention, and resources to putting defenses in place to keep "the bad guys" out. But the ongoing need to protect against outside attackers makes it easy for organizations to lose sight of another, even more potent threat to security: the bad guys from within. Understanding which assets should be protected and who should be allowed to access them is also a complex undertaking often overlooked in the enterprise.

Industry analysts estimate that 70 to 80 percent of security breaches are caused by insiders.[1] Sometimes, these events are due to people who fully intend to do bad things for their own gain. Just look at the number of insider-related security events that have made headlines in recent years. Employees have managed to steal millions from employers or have compromised, used, or sold the identities of co-workers and customers.

How did they do it? By accessing data, systems, and equipment—freely and often repeatedly—that should have been off limits to them. They were able to take advantage of a situation where their actions simply were not monitored effectively, or at all, by anyone else in the organization.

Insider fraud is costly and embarrassing for companies. But truthfully, these events are not as frequent as incidents caused by well-meaning people who end up doing things that compromise network and data security. These are the other "bad guys" who pose a serious threat: careless employees who lose laptops in airport terminals or have them stolen from their cars. Trusting people who, without a thought, will follow a link in an email they believe is from a reputable source but that leads them to a malware-laden site that infects their company's entire network. Workers who, in the interest of collaborating more efficiently, ignore company policy and load documents onto an Internet file-sharing site. And later, that confidential information is copied by a disgruntled co-worker who takes a job with a competitor.

The dramatic and near-overnight change brought about by the global financial crisis that began to unfold in 2007 with an astounding number of layoffs across industries added a new dimension to the data security challenge: How much data has been leaving with these employees—accidentally or intentionally? C-level executives should wonder who in the organization is responsible for data security and immediately take away access rights and collect equipment from departing employees. Unfortunately, there is a good chance that at most organizations no one has this responsibility.

The consumerization of IT, increasing use of mobile devices and Web 2.0 applications, and greater reliance on remote workforces and third-party service providers make data loss—the type that can lead not only to embarrassment, but also reputation damage and financial loss—more than just a possibility for today's organizations. It's a very real threat.

One Breach, Multiple Shockwaves

Of course, criminals delight in how easy modern technology makes their mission of compromising and then utilizing sensitive data for financial gain. As we explored in earlier chapters, shady characters around the globe are building a thriving business developing and deploying ever-more sophisticated tools and strategies to access or outright steal data from companies, or dupe trusting and unsuspecting individuals into simply handing it over.

Data loss sounds benign, but it can be devastating for victims. Just one breach can touch millions of people worldwide and take years to completely play out or be resolved.

According to the Privacy Rights Clearinghouse, which maintains a "Chronology of Data Breaches," 250 million personal records have been reported lost or stolen since January 2005—just in the United States. And the Identity Theft Resource Center (ITRC) says reported data breaches nearly doubled in 2008 from 2007—which, by the way, had itself exceeded the total reported for 2006. ITRC says financial institutions were responsible for more than half of the 35 million personal records known to be lost or exposed during 2008.

The infamous data breach of 2005 involving TJX, parent company of retail chains such as TJ Maxx and Marshalls, remains the largest single theft of consumer information. Tens of millions of credit card numbers, and sensitive personal information such as Social Security numbers (SSN), belonging to hundreds of thousands of individuals were compromised due to the use of WEP (Wired Equivalent Privacy) wireless security. It is estimated that the incident cost TJX more than US$1 billion, and the company suffered serious damage to its reputation.

In 2009, data breach activity got off to an impressive start when a leading credit card processor in the United States revealed that it discovered and contained malware in its processing system that might have been "the result of a widespread global cyber fraud operation." Officials with that company have not disclosed how many consumer records might have been compromised in the incident, but given that the company processes cards for approximately 250,000 businesses in the United States, the number of people affected could easily be in the millions. (A few months later, it was reported that the hacker responsible for the TJX incident was also indicted in this case, and other data breaches involving major retailers.)[2]

Although these are two high-profile cases, data loss is quite commonplace today and can be costly for companies: The Ponemon Institute estimates that in 2008, data breaches cost U.S. companies, on average, US$6.65 million, with the largest cost increase being lost business.

More businesses—some proactively, and even more reactively—are now realizing their data is a vital asset that must be protected. Many have implemented data loss prevention (DLP) programs to help keep data secure, whether it is stored, in use, or moving around the network.

Companies employ an array of tools and strategies as part of DLP, including encryption. PricewaterhouseCoopers' "2008 Global State of Information Security Study" reports more organizations are encrypting sensitive information on laptops, which are primary contributors to data loss because they are easily lost or stolen. Encryption is also used on databases, file shares, backup tapes, and removable media.

The report also cites growing use of web/Internet capabilities such as content-filtering, website certification/accreditation and secure browsers, and technologies that protect wireless devices and tools by discovering unauthorized devices or preventing intrusions.

Despite these efforts, security incidents related to data loss are on the rise. Some data loss is due to online criminals phishing and using malware. Some is the result of hackers breaking into weak or unsecured systems and devices. Much of it, though, is accidental. With more mobile and handheld devices on the work scene, there are more opportunities for employees to lose equipment containing sensitive data or logon information. And in today's Web 2.0 environment, information is shared between people inside and outside of an organization more often and in an unsecured fashion.

According to the Cisco 2008 report, "The Challenge of Data Leakage for Businesses and Employees Around the World," 44 percent of employees share work devices with others without supervision. Meanwhile, 18 percent share passwords with co-workers. These users likely think nothing of the threat to the organization—or themselves—that they create by exposing sensitive data through their careless use of technology. But there are also those who mean to do harm, and their ranks appear to be multiplying.

Insiders

Fraud, hacking, and identity theft by insiders are real security threats, which can be especially damaging for an organization. Insiders know security weaknesses and how best to exploit them.

How much damage can one person do? Just look at French bank Société Générale. In 2008, a bank employee who was a trader admitted that by engaging in unauthorized stock market deals, he had caused a €4.9 billion loss for the financial institution.

The employee used knowledge and experience he had gained through previous work in the bank's risk management office to conceal his losses through falsified transactions. His fraudulent activity—which required a breach of five layers of control and included the theft of computer access codes—was discovered, eventually, by auditors looking into an error made by the bank's chairman and CEO.

And then there's beleaguered mortgage lender Countrywide Financial—a company that did not need more bad press following the subprime debacle: According to FBI reports, a senior financial analyst in the company's subprime mortgage division spent Sunday nights during the summer of 2008 knitting himself a golden parachute of sorts. He copied more than 2 million customer records to personal flash drives and then sold the sensitive information to identity thieves. This might have made for a nice retirement nest egg, had he and his accomplice not been found out and arrested.

These high-profile cases of insiders participating in data theft are stunning examples of the cost to an organization, and its customers, due to the action of just one rogue employee. But more widespread—and harder to detect—are the mundane threats, such as employees taking customer lists or product plans out the door when they leave the company.

Of all the data breaches involving financial institutions in 2008, insiders were at the heart of nearly one-quarter of all *known* incidents, according to ITRC. In today's weak economy, in which many employees have lost their jobs or become dissatisfied with their work situation, and where budgets available to address security concerns are smaller, insider threats—and their likelihood of success—are of increasing concern. In addition, as companies cut costs, they might increase their dependence on teleworkers, consultants, and third-party resources. This can be cost-effective but requires additional security policies and implementations to work securely at the edges of an organization's network.

Adding to concerns about insider threats, larger entities such as competing corporations and hostile governments—and organized crime—have been placing agents within organizations they want to compromise. Therefore, insider threats can be expected to remain a major security concern for businesses of all types.

Compliance Pitfall

Legislation and industry initiatives for making data on networks more secure and informing those affected by data breaches are increasing worldwide. Today, there are thousands of laws, regulations and standards—just in the United States—related to data management.

The Health Insurance Portability and Accountability Act (HIPAA) and the Payment Card Industry Data Security Standard (PCI DSS) are two well-known examples. Laws and regulations such as these require, among other things, encryption of personal information on laptops, PDAs, and portable media, including flash drives; encryption of personal information transmitted over the Internet; development and publication of SSN privacy protection policies; and specific measures to protect the confidentiality and security of personally identifiable information (PII) like SSNs.

Although many regulatory standards are designed to help protect PII, organizations should never view compliance as a security blanket. Being "compliant" comes down to checking boxes on a standardized form. And by focusing solely on achieving compliance, organizations lose sight of other, potentially more serious risks to their sensitive data, including financial information and intellectual property. Multiple security incidents in 2008 involved organizations that were considered "compliant."

Compliance procedures are intended to help organizations achieve specific objectives that mitigate only certain security risks. But most do not and cannot address today's array of web-based applications, virtualization technologies, social networking tools, and related security vulnerabilities and threats, which online cybercriminals increasingly target.

DLP: Chasing Rainbows?

It has been said that DLP solutions are a bit like anti-aging cream. The value proposition is irresistible to corporations, but many of the solutions don't really live up to the hype. However, with both DLP and anti-aging cream, even a partial solution is still valuable. To get value from a DLP solution, companies must recognize that they cannot protect all their data from all threats. They also must realize that they don't have to. Building policies and tools that focus on a narrow set of extremely high-value data can yield great results.

"Companies need to figure out first what it is they need to protect—what data is most critical to the organization," says Scott Olechowski, director of Product Strategy and Business Development for Cisco. "Then, they need to understand the risks. If they don't, they are not going to solve anything, no matter how many policies or how much technology they throw at the problem."

Many companies have had great success identifying small clusters of high-value data and scanning outbound network traffic for traces of this data. There are a handful of advanced DLP policy tools that will extract "fingerprints" or create rules that allow for accurate detection of the most sensitive data, say a press release or new design document, with a manageably low false positive rate.

Furthermore, with the recent advances in network-based processing, it is feasible to scan for this data using advanced rule sets such as proximity analysis and fingerprinting on real-time protocols such as web and IM traffic. This has significant potential. Being able to catch just one instance of a press release leaving the company before it is officially released can be worth a significant amount to the company.

The technology to make this possible without disrupting the end-user experience has finally arrived. However, none of these things can prevent data loss entirely, just as anti-malware technology cannot stop all attacks, and acceptable use policies (AUPs) cannot guarantee 100 percent adherence from every single employee all the time. But the "ideal" security policy for the Web 2.0 work environment *should* encompass this security-strengthening triumvirate—antimalware, AUPs, and DLP. Yet even when working in tandem, these things are not enough to enable employees to collaborate anytime, anywhere, from any device securely. In fact, right now it is fair to say that collaboration *without* confidence is in full swing.

Endnotes

[1] "Insider Hacker Activity," by Karen Hirschhorn, *IT Defense*, December/January 2007.

[2] "TJX Hacker Charged with Heartland, Hannaford Breaches," By Kim Zetter, *Wired*, August 17, 2009. http://www.wired.com/threatlevel/2009/08/tjx-hacker-charged-with-heartland/.

References

Cisco 2008 Annual Security Report.
http://www.cisco.com/en/US/prod/collateral/vpndevc/securityreview12-2.pdf.

Cisco 2009 Annual Security Report.
http://www.cisco.com/en/US/prod/collateral/vpndevc/cisco_2009_asr.pdf.

"The Challenge of Data Leakage For Businesses and Employees Around the World."
http://www.cisco.com/en/US/solutions/collateral/ns170/ns896/ns895/Cisco_STL_Data_
Leakage_2008_PR1.pdf.

"Data Loss Prevention Best Practices," IronPort Systems.
http://www.ironport.com/pdf/ironport_dlp_booklet.pdf.

Pricewaterhousecoopers, "Global State of Information Security Survey."
http://www.pwc.com.

McGlasson, Linda, "Identity Theft: Lender Countrywide's Insider Case,"
Bankinfosecurity.com, August 14, 2008.
http://www.bankinfosecurity.com/articles.php?art_id=937.

Identity Theft Resource Center, "ITRC 2008 Breach List."
http://www.idtheftcenter.org/artman2/publish/lib_survey/ITRC_2008_Breach_List.shtml.

Ponemon, Larry, "Cost of a Data Breach: Can You Afford $6.65 Million?"
ComputerWorld.com, February 4, 2009.
http://www.computerworld.com/action/article.do?command=viewArticleBasic&articleId
=9127376.

Privacy Rights Clearinghouse, "A Chronology of Data Breaches."
http://www.privacyrights.org/ar/ChronDataBreaches.htm#1.

"Heartland Payment Systems Uncovers Malicious Software In Its Processing System. No
merchant information or cardholder Social Security numbers compromised," Heartland
Payment Systems press release, January 20, 2009.
http://www.2008breach.com/PressReleases.asp.

Chapter 13

Collaboration Without Confidence

This chapter includes the following topics:

- Saying "No Thanks" to the "Culture of No"

- One Workforce, Different Needs

- Secure Collaboration: Anytime, Anywhere, from Any Device

- Countervailing Forces

Policies are vital security measures, but they have obvious limitations—namely, their inability to directly control the behavior of human beings.

As the consumerization of IT trend demonstrates, and Cisco's research underscores, when it comes to technology, employees often bend or break the rules to do what they want or accomplish what they have been asked to do more quickly and efficiently. The focus is on getting the job done using the best tools available, and workers are often unaware that they rely on only a thin and porous safety net to protect them, and their employer, from a security mishap.

However, organizations should take comfort in knowing their policies—provided they are well thought-out, clearly communicated and effectively enforced—can enhance work-force productivity while also reducing freewheeling behavior by employees. In the best case, an intelligent security policy can make an insider think twice before committing fraud. In short, carefully crafted and reasonable policies make people less inclined to break the rules.

However, because even the most progressive policies cannot prevent every adverse event that results from an employee's irresponsibility or determination to commit a crime, many organizations tend to view their policies as "CYA" (that is, cover-your-you-know-what) insurance more than tools for educating and empowering their workers. If someone makes a serious mistake or commits a crime that embarrasses the company and puts it in legal hot water, management can say, "Well, we told him not to do that. He signed a form his first week on the job saying he understood and would follow the rules. So, really, you shouldn't sue us."

The CYA factor is one reason why many companies end up adopting a "culture of no" in which policies are purposefully—and stiflingly—strict. But by saying no to everything new or different from what represents "normal" for the organization, many companies believe they are controlling, or at least slowing down, their employees' adoption of new technology. In the absurd, the most secure computer is the unplugged computer.

Control is just an illusion, however. Think about the U.K.-based advertising and marketing firm discussed in Chapter 11, "Acceptable Use Policies": Several work teams—and some of the agency's clients—had been collaborating via Google Apps for some time without management's knowledge or approval. Only when the agency's IT department amped up its acceptable use policy "to block the whole download category" was it discovered that this activity was going on and would be difficult to stop because the work had progressed so far.

Part of the problem is that organizations, by nature, don't make snap or sweeping policy decisions with the exception of denying something. Their bureaucratic wheels just don't roll fast enough to keep up with the pace of change in technology and the rate at which users embrace new things. Companies want to control the clock, and take as much time as they feel is needed to thoroughly consider proposed changes, weigh costs and benefits, run test groups, evaluate results, decide on the if, how, and when of a policy change, and then officially institute and communicate that change throughout the organization. The majority of corporate IT teams view new ideas or technologies as yet more projects that consume an already limited budget.

However, technology adoption by users in the Web 2.0 world is so rapid that this process is outdated. It is reminiscent of the late 20th century "Should we let our employees have access to the Internet?" mentality. As previously discussed, this painfully slow approach to giving the green light and allowing employees to use new technology and devices causes "necessary noncompliance" by users with the policies intended to protect them and the organization. When they know what works best for them, they simply can't reconcile their preferences with their employers' policies. And often, what they want *is* good for the organization, even if the company is not ready to accept change.

IT blogger Scott Wilson had this warning for CIOs in a 2009 posting for his "The Vision Thing" blog on CIO-weblog.com: "Don't let your users get ahead of you on the technology curve. There are good, time-tested reasons that they may not understand which may compel you to insist on particular solutions or restrictions...but you have to avoid your IT department becoming a 'culture of no' and driving users into the arms of Web 2.0 providers...who could care less about your security and efficiency problems."

Instead, Wilson recommends that IT be a "trusted partner" that recognizes "this new state of affairs" and "becomes the delivery mechanism for [Web 2.0] tools." He writes, "These are just tools; good or evil is how you use them."[1]

Unfortunately, though, the "good and evil" decision is not purely in the hands of the user. Whether a company is ultimately accepting of its employees using Web 2.0 technology or the handheld devices they personally prefer, trouble still lurks from beyond the organization's security perimeter.

An example of how quickly and quietly bad things can happen before they are detected took place in early 2009. Internet security firm Tiversa revealed that sometime in the summer of 2008, an unauthorized peer-to-peer (P2P) file-sharing program installed on an employee's PC had led to a security breach. Blueprints "including planned engineering upgrades, avionic schematics, and computer network information" for the U.S. president's helicopter, Marine One, had been transferred to an IP address in Tehran, Iran. According to Tiversa, the address belonged to an "information concentrator"—someone who searches P2P networks for sensitive information.

Most organizations are, understandably, desperate not to become the latest headline involving a technology-related security breach, which is why they are protective of their "culture of no." But in addition to the relentless push and pull of the consumerization of IT, the benefits of Web 2.0 are also becoming increasingly more difficult for companies to ignore—especially as they look to compete and succeed in a post-global recession business environment. Organizations will be looking for ways to attract and retain top talent from the Gen Y demographic pool, and to maintain or increase the productivity of their entire workforce while also controlling costs.

Saying "No Thanks" to the "Culture of No"

Web 2.0 is not only changing the nature of work, but also where people want to work. This is driven largely by the expectations of ultrawired Gen Y. However, many companies don't yet see a direct connection between embracing Web 2.0 today and having a more productive, highly competitive workforce tomorrow. Some organizations are noticing, though, that their stance on Web 2.0 access is coming up as a topic in job interviews with Gen Y candidates, right along with questions about salary and benefits.

In an interview with U.K.-based *Computing* magazine in early 2008, Duncan Scott, chief information officer for global property services firm DTZ Holdings, said Web 2.0 is "so important" yet "not understood at a boardroom level." He added, "We have students asking us what our policy is toward Web 2.0, and unless we embrace it, we will be unable to attract the best talent. We have to face...that the new generation will throw current working practices into the bin. Restricting access to unwanted sites is prudent, but out-of-date security management practices should not prevent new ways of doing business."[2]

Think about the challenges at Australian private school, Wesley College, discussed in Chapter 11. Network services manager Russell Graham told of the acceptable use policies all students sign—and then never reference. Wesley College does not permit students to access popular social networking sites, but the children circumvent the rules time and again with anonymous proxies they share with each other. (Graham says students are downloading *1.5 terabytes* of data monthly from the Internet via the school's connection.) And the kids do their best to gain access to forbidden areas and information on the school's network. "Students have been using network-sniffing tools to monitor and capture any data of interest, such as passwords, emails, and files," says Graham. "They spend their lunch hours trying to discover any potential vulnerabilities in our environments."

These students represent the next-generation workforce and are clearly even more loath to accept a "culture of no" than their Gen Y colleagues already in the business world. But older Millennials aren't exactly taking "no" for an answer, either.

A major auto insurance provider in the United States is already seeing how denying its more than 20,000 employees access to Web 2.0 applications and social networking sites is having a direct impact on employee retention. "This is starting to show up in exit interviews," says the company's head of IT. "We have associates leaving just six months after joining us, and they tell us, 'You guys seemed so tech-savvy from the outside, but when we got here, we found out we can't even IM our friends and family to let them know we're going to be home late.' These are real multitaskers who want to stay in constant contact. What they want to do is common practice today, we know, but trying to convince a very conservative and mature company that this is possible is a very difficult thing to do."

But it's not just Gen Y pushing the envelope on policy. Take a California high-tech company that, in the interest of security, discourages on-the-job social networking by its thousands of employees worldwide. However, despite the strict rules, some departments, and employees who work within the executive ranks, are often given more latitude, according to a systems engineer and project manager for the company.

"Some upper-level executives have been looking at Gen Y apps and have started leveraging sites like Facebook and MySpace," he says. "Recently, one of our people wanted to download a web program that went against our policy. But we had to allow it because that person works in the office of the company president. It's like, what do you say?"

The systems engineer admits that the company's policy is a bit of a double standard. "Our marketing and human resources people also use Facebook to find new employees and brand the company. And LinkedIn is an unofficial networking tool for many of us here," he says. "Even though we discourage our employees from using these tools, as a company, we need them to grow. But it really is like telling your kids not to watch too much TV and then watching too much yourself."

However, he adds that even without the (begrudgingly given) blessing from IT, there are plenty of employees, companywide, who are bending the rules to make sure they are keeping one foot in the Web 2.0 world while on the job. "As a company, we don't allow instant messaging—things like AIM and Skype," he explains. "We've deemed them to be too insecure. But I bet about 75 percent of our employees have those types of applications on their PCs, even though they are not supposed to."

There's a double standard at work at the auto insurance provider, too, according to the company's head of IT. He admits, "We allow a small subset of employees—executives and knowledge workers, mostly—to have access to webmail even though the company has a denial policy."

He adds that "over-productive associates" are also a concern for the organization. "They want to work from home, and use their own email system to send company-related data over the Internet to their home machines," he says. "But our policy does not allow that. Yet we've found many supervisors doing the same kind of thing by transferring data over to unencrypted thumb drives—again, simply in the interest of doing work. It's a problem that's kind of hard to get your arms around. You want to enable your employees to be as productive as possible, but you also have to enforce your policies."

One Workforce, Diverse Needs

Although employees not adhering to policies has IT departments working overtime to keep the organization secure, the demands of mobile and remote workers make the problems even worse. But companies do their best to keep tight reins on these types of employees, too; for example, by permitting use of only "approved" mobile and handheld devices, mandating encryption of sensitive data when it is transmitted or stored, or insisting that they access the company network only through a secure connection, such as a secure socket layer virtual private network (SSL VPN). However, this "system" has so many moving parts that even the most well-staffed and experienced IT departments struggle to monitor security risks.

"We have a huge number of remote users accessing our network," says the security engineer for a not-for-profit Midwest healthcare company. "We know our data is encrypted, but we don't know how much information, including patient information, is going out [of the network]."

He continues, "We're kind of at a crossroads with mobility—whether to support devices like the iPhone. We support the BlackBerry within the organization, but we have more than 1000 physicians and about the same number of practitioners working out in the field who want to use their own mobile devices, like the iPhone or iTouch, which we don't support. They don't understand our policy because they don't realize the potential for data loss and security compromises by using unsupported devices."

The California-based high-tech company also recently went "BlackBerry enterprisewide" according to its systems engineer, but the policy change affects only about 30 percent of the company's employees—those who are permitted to use handheld devices in their job. But he says the organization is not yet ready for the iPhone—or even some of the newer BlackBerry devices. "One of the most important considerations for us is having the ability to wipe a device anytime from anywhere."

Although the company supports the BlackBerry, it has put tight security policies in place on those devices to control "the proliferation of Web 2.0 applications," according to the systems engineer. "The devices have to be unlocked by us in order for certain things to be downloaded," he adds. "That's really the one big gotcha with mobile devices—all of these add-ons, these Web 2.0 applications."

Some organizations make no apologies for having strict policies about what devices they support and tight controls on data and network access, especially when they need to worry about regulatory compliance. "Sure, there can be lots of demand from employees who want to use their own mobile devices, like the iPhone, but we just don't do it," says the head of IT for a global healthcare services and products organization with more than 90,000 employees worldwide, many of them remote or mobile workers.

"We don't hire employees for their ability to get to an office," he adds. "Our nurse practitioners, for example—we need to put them wherever they are needed. That might be a rural area that has a hospital, but isn't large enough for us to put an office there. A fair amount of our employees are telecommuters; some are completely home-based. They connect to the Internet via a broadband connection and use a VPN client to communicate with us. We provide the equipment and the telecom line."

He continues, "Our mobile workforce includes our sales professionals, who are running around with laptops and tablets that are mandated to be secured. And every machine 'out in the wild' must have full disk-level encryption—no exceptions. Local encryption on mobile devices is actually the law in a couple of states where we operate. No unencrypted personal health information on mobile devices whatsoever—thumb drives, laptops, cell phones."

We've found that the BlackBerry meets our encryption requirement and we can enforce it through the Blackberry Enterprise Server. So, we turn it on, and only allow address books to be unencrypted," he adds.

Meanwhile, the auto insurance company does not support the BlackBerry. According to the company's head of IT, "We do use Windows mobile devices, but only about 260 executives and knowledge workers have them—no line or field workers. Most devices are company-issued, but our associates can choose their own device if they are willing to give up their rights to manage it and pay for their own service."

And does he expect the organization to move away from the "culture of no" and allow its "line and field workers" to use a handheld device while on the job?

"I absolutely see that changing over the next five years," he says. "In fact, I think the handheld device will be the only device our adjusters in the field use. That just makes sense—especially from a productivity standpoint."

Secure Collaboration: Anytime, Anywhere, from Any Device

Deciding what technology to support and how to support it and then implementing it requires a great deal of time and energy for IT and company management. So, too, does creating and enforcing policies around those decisions.

Antimalware, acceptable use policies, and data loss prevention will all play key roles in security policies of the future. To be effective and create benefits for an organization by not working against employees' efforts to work more productively, these policies need to avoid the "culture of no" and embrace new technologies that are user-friendly and allow workers to get their jobs done more efficiently.

However, the tools available for enforcing these forward-looking policies are quite limited today. Organizations are desperately seeking tools that enable them to create policies of openness that encourage collaboration, but still protect their valuable intellectual property.

Organizations should be striving to create an environment in which people can communicate and collaborate with each other using the tools, devices, and technologies that best suit their needs, and where they, and the businesses they work for, can feel confident the information they create and exchange is secure.

Cisco is actively working toward this security vision by building a system that enables its customers to collaborate with confidence. The companies interviewed for this book are diverse in size, the nature of their business, and the makeup of their workforce, but their stories reveal they are united in common security challenges presented by the consumerization of IT, Web 2.0 technology, and mobility.

The quandaries they face are also shared by security-minded companies worldwide. Consider the following Web 2.0 dilemmas, which could apply to myriad organizations across the globe:

> A chief executive officer of a financial services firm traveling in Asia opens an e-card she believes was sent by a friend. However, it's actually part of a targeted malware attack. The email with the e-card contains a link that leads the CEO to a fake website that downloads malware to her laptop. The malware then scans the laptop for documents containing the word "earnings."

How could this malware attack have been prevented?

> A marketing executive is looking for an old contact who might provide insight into a potential client's business needs. He's on the road and wants to use his company-issued handheld device to search a social networking site for the contact's profile.

How can the company allow the executive to access that site while also preventing him from posting his company email address on the site for any spammer or hacker to harvest?

> Sales team members for a medical devices manufacturer are encouraged by their employer to work on building new leads in a high-potential geographic market using customer data hosted by a SaaS provider.

How can the company ensure salespeople who are no longer employees do not access the customer lists in the hosted SaaS application? Even more important, how can they log, capture, or inspect the access to this data when users are going directly to the SaaS app from handheld devices somewhere on the Internet?

An aerospace company has developed a new turbine design. They are using a shared workspace application to collaborate with the airframe manufacturer.

How can the company ensure the CAD drawing and design specifications do not get posted in the shared workspace where a third party might access it?

A bank wants to use a wiki to update its employees on the state of the business and share plans to take advantage of new business opportunities when the economy is firmly in recovery.

How can the bank ensure this information is easily accessible to employees but does not get into the hands of competitors or the press?

Situations just like these, and countless others, occur every moment of every day in a world where users can access business-critical information—financial data, sales reports, legal contracts, intellectual property, customers' personal information, and more—directly from the Internet using a handheld device.

Countervailing Forces

Security policies and the tools to enforce them are entering a period of profound change driven by two countervailing forces. First, there is the trend toward openness. The use of Web 2.0 applications is unstoppable, but it also will yield significant productivity enhancements for corporations. This means data is on the move—from outside the traditional well-protected "fortress" of the corporate data center into the ether of the Internet cloud.

At the same time, users are on the move. Handheld computing and the consumerization of IT mean more users are accessing more data from more places in the network and from more, different platforms than ever before. In the current environment, the worst-case scenario for a corporate security practitioner is the intersection of mobility and SaaS. When an executive accesses Salesforce.com from her iPhone, for example, there is no traditional firewall in that transaction. So, the question that must be answered is: How does the IT team manage, monitor, inspect, log, or control access to this sensitive information?

Although companies are being either pushed or pulled into a posture of openness to embrace mobility and Web 2.0, the need for an advanced security policy is greater than ever. Malware is getting smarter and harder to stop. And regulatory requirements continue to grow in importance.

Meanwhile, it is becoming increasingly obvious that acceptable use policies must progress beyond a simple "no to everything" approach and instead articulate meaningful boundaries in the Web 2.0 world that enable efficiencies but still protect users and data. And as the underlying technology continues to mature, it is becoming quite reasonable for companies to contemplate data protection policies that keep their sensitive information safe and secure but do not limit its usefulness.

These countervailing forces of the trend toward openness and the need for greater security are highlighting the need for a significant evolution of the tools businesses use to enforce polices. Security must move away from the hub-and-spoke model in which all traffic is backhauled to a small number of egress points in which security devices— "magic black boxes"—are resident.

The new security architecture must live in the cloud and on premises. It needs to have capabilities to understand and interpret content in email, web, and IM—all major communication protocols. It must understand Web 2.0 applications, so it can distinguish Skype from Facebook and Salesforce.com. And it needs to be always on, always available, and always fast.

Most important, the new security architecture for the borderless network must improve the end-user experience. As history shows, if security gets in the way of end users, it will find a way around it. But if a security architecture can make the end-user experience *better*, everyone wins.

The Cisco vision is to create an end-user experience of being always on, always connected, no matter where the user might be. At the office or the sandwich shop around the corner or at an airport on the other side of the globe, what is needed is a new security architecture that can yield a consistent and excellent end-user experience, in which users have full access to data and applications but are also fully controlled.

This is not a small task to accomplish. But the underlying silicon and software technologies have progressed to the point where it is feasible that it can be done.

Endnotes

[1] "The complex reality of end-user application development," by Scott Wilson, March 6, 2009, CIO-weblog.com. http://www.cio-weblog.com/50226711/the_complex_reality_of_enduser_application_development.php.

[2] "Security that's fit for business," By Lisa Kelly, Computing, March 10, 2009. http://www.computing.co.uk/computing/features/2238144/security-fit-business-4507361.

References

Cisco 2008 Annual Security Report.
http://www.cisco.com/en/US/prod/collateral/vpndevc/securityreview12-2.pdf.

Cisco 2009 Annual Security Report.
http://cisco.com/en/US/prod/collateral/vpndevc/cisco_2009_asr.pdf.

"Classified data on president's helicopter leaked via P2P, found on Iranian computer," by
Jaikumar Vijayan, *ComputerWorld*, March 2, 2009.
http://www.computerworld.com/action/article.do?command=
viewArticleBasic&taxonomyName=government&articleId=9128820&taxonomyId=
13&intsrc=kc_top.

"Data Leakage Worldwide: The Effectiveness of Security Policies."
http://www.cisco.com/en/US/solutions/collateral/ns170/ns896/ns895/white_paper_c11-
503131.html.

"Data on Marine One Found on Iranian Computer Network," The Aero-News Network,
March 2, 2009. http://www.aero-news.net/index.cfm?ContentBlockID=28502da9-73cb-
43f8-ae9a-71e205a4af2a.

Chapter 14

Identity Management: We Need to Know if You Are a Dog

This chapter includes the following topics:

■   Identity: The Key to the Security Kingdom

■   Establishing Identity

■   A Flexible Identity Fabric

The New Yorker once ran a cartoon that featured a dog sitting at a computer keyboard. The caption read, "On the Internet, nobody knows you're a dog." (See Figure 14-1.) This simple cartoon captures the heart of a problem that costs enterprises billions of dollars. Identity is the foundation of any security policy—who are you and what are you allowed to do? However, the onset of the "borderless enterprise" and Web 2.0 makes the simple task of distinguishing between employees, business partners, clients—and even dogs— much more complicated than it was a decade ago.

In the late 1990s and early 2000s, the network was a fairly static configuration of physi- cal equipment used to mark clear divisions between what was accessible "inside" and "outside" the corporate perimeter. As such, security policies typically relied on a physical infrastructure to define identity and policy. For instance, an accountant would be assigned to the finance subnet of the corporate network and would have access to finance applications on that subnet. A developer would be assigned to the engineering subnet and could access source code stored on that subnet. And a random Internet user would have no access to any of these applications or data.

As businesses embrace collaboration and globalization, the hard connection between pol- icy and physical infrastructure becomes strained. To transact business without borders, we need security policies that express simple ideas about which workers can access which applications and data, without being hard-wired to IP addresses, subnets, and the complex infrastructure that powers all networks.

In short, security can no longer be tied inextricably to the physical infrastructure under- neath it. The unconstrained access to information we seek requires an advanced security system that abstracts the underlying network fabric. This system needs to enable businesses to express policies in terms of who a user is, what applications he or she uses, and what content he or she accesses. It must work both inside and outside the traditional corporate network to meet the security challenges of today's decentralized and highly collaborative work environment. And it must enable an enterprise that transcends borders, where users, assets, and critical information are all protected.

This intelligent security system is what will allow us to collaborate with confidence.

"On the Internet, nobody knows you're a dog."

Figure 14-1

Identity: The Key to the Security Kingdom

Establishing identity is a core challenge to Internet security. Today's highly sophisticated cybercriminals can easily conceal their true identities and appear to unsuspecting users as trusted entities. And they can shed their skins and reappear elsewhere online as something or someone else "reputable" within moments. The lack of a lasting identity online enables shape-shifting criminals to operate with impunity.

This is the world we live in on the Internet. As we saw in Chapter 8, "The Bad Guys from Outside: Malware," modern malware such as the Storm virus can switch from sending spam to hosting malware to launching a SQL injection attack on a web server every 5 or 10 minutes. Modern attacks like this can dynamically change their IP address and therefore, abandon their previous identity. They can readily find ways to mimic or hijack the identity of a legitimate entity on the Internet.

Vint Cerf, a scientist widely regarded as the "Father of the Internet," summed up this frustrating situation on a recent Twitter post about the Internet: "We don't authenticate very well."[1] If we had the opportunity to build the Internet all over again, we'd build authentication into the core of the system.

Meanwhile, in the enterprise, you might assume that identifying the "good guys" who are accessing the network, such as employees, business partners, and clients, would be a straightforward task, and that making sure these users access only appropriate information would be a deterministic and reliable process. But they aren't. Determining user identity and access in today's enterprise environment is a complex undertaking.

In yesterday's enterprise, employees would come into the office, turn on their desktop computers, and interact primarily with approved resources on their own corporate network or subnetwork such as database servers, printers, and backup systems. In this cut-and-dry environment, it made sense to have identity revolve mainly around IP addresses and boxes on the network.

In the forward-looking enterprise, employees, contractors, and other third parties access the network using laptops or smartphones from wherever they might be—their office, their home, a hotel, or a client site. They might constantly switch devices and the points of origin from which they work. The devices in use in the enterprise are increasingly a mix of corporate and noncorporate-issued, which adds to the complexity. In addition to resources that live on-site at the office, today's workers need access to web-based applications that might reside outside of the traditional perimeter.

"The collaboration technologies in use today demand stronger identity management," says John Stewart, Cisco chief security officer. "You need to collaborate with confidence with people within and outside of your organization. And as you're using more and more web-based services to work and collaborate, identity becomes the key to the kingdom."

It no longer makes sense to have identity revolve around the IP address someone happens to be logging in from or a network box. Now, identity needs to be about the actual users and their activities. Differentiating between users and their levels of access and control is essential to enterprise security. Security systems and policies must be smart enough to detect who a user is, no matter what device he or she uses or from where he or she logs in.

At the same time, it is important to know what points of entry exist on the network, and to authenticate devices connected to the network. Enterprise networks have become much larger, more complex, and more distributed. Furthermore, more types of devices and boxes connect to the network than ever before. Knowing what device lives where, and setting policies for the types of actions a device can perform, are vital to network security.

Therefore, the next-generation security solution requires that we move away from the current system using IP address, port, and protocol as the basis for policy and move toward tomorrow's security architecture, which will have a directed, oriented policy at its core. This intelligent security solution will enable a business to easily express the relatively simple policy of "Fred can access finance information and Candice can access CAD drawings, but Fred cannot access CAD drawings and Candice cannot access finance apps."

In today's complex networking environment, a simple policy like this can translate into hundreds of access control rules and authentication steps—and a large operational burden to maintain it going forward. Many customers today have firewalls that contain more than 500,000 rules, an amount too difficult for a human being to manage practically. Many security professionals feel these rule sets have ballooned to the point where they are completely unmanageable. And although the person who wrote the rules in the first place might be gone from the organization, everyone is afraid to touch them for fear of disrupting the enterprise.

To reduce this complexity, the security architecture of tomorrow must operate at a higher level. If today's IP, port, and protocol constructs are similar to assembly language programming, tomorrow's application-, identity-, and content-based policies are similar to C programming. Borderless enterprise security will be a more powerful tool-set to compactly and flexibly express enterprise business rules.

Identity is the foundation of this system, and it is the common language that will enable businesses large and small to collaborate with confidence.

Establishing Identity

When employees join an organization today, they're typically assigned a badge, an email address, a username, and a password—the building blocks of identity in the enterprise. Some organizations go even further and ask users to authenticate to a network or company-owned resource with a hardware or software token, such as an encrypted single-sign-on key or a biometric fingerprint scanner. When the user's identity has been initially established, policies defining the type of access appropriate for the user in different circumstances and at different times can be set.

In theory, this should be simple and easy—but it's not. Identity has been onerous and complicated to manage due to issues with different protocols, policies, ports, devices, and legacy systems colliding. One IT leader in a company with a workforce of 60,000 was told to find the "single source of truth"—the master corporate identity store that had a listing of all employees and their access levels. Instead, he found 15 "single" sources of truth—a highly complex web to maintain and synchronize.

Even the fundamental need to establish identity wasn't always clear. When corporate networks were simpler, smaller and less distributed, and based around the notion that employees' desktop computers would be plugged into an Ethernet port by IT staff and stay there, it seemed logical to base identity around MAC and IP addresses. For example, Ethernet ports, because they were inside the office building, must be, by definition, in use by employees. Therefore, in the past, establishing exactly which employee was using a port and exactly when a port was in use and for how long didn't seem important.

Today, however, employees might use desktops but also (and even more often) laptops and smartphones to wirelessly access corporate resources. That means their identity and permitted access level need to be established whenever they log on, and in many cases an extra layer of security, such as a virtual private network (VPN) or encryption, is used.

At the same time, people plugged into an Ethernet port at the headquarters office building might not all be employees; some might be guests or contractors. You need to provide them with enough access to be productive but not so much that they can wander through employee-only areas of the network at will.

As Pat Calhoun, chief technology officer of the Ethernet and Wireless Technology Group at Cisco, says, "More and more guests and customers and partners are coming into the enterprise and in some cases are just plugging into any Ethernet port they find. So, there's a big focus on applying the learning about strong authentication from wireless networks to wired networks, and creating a common security profile for each user for both wired and wireless networks."

Wireless Network Versus Wired Network Identity Management   During the rise of the wireless LAN as a productivity tool over the last decade, IT staff and vendors realized from the get-go that access control and authentication of devices trying to connect wirelessly to the network would be crucial. To enable smooth authentication and access, network access control standards—such as 802.1x—were established and "baked in" to wirelessly enabled devices.

However, at the earlier time when wired networks were widely deployed, anytime-anywhere-by-any-device access hadn't been commonly envisioned, so identity-based network access control standards were not baked in. Instead, access control took place on multiple boxes on the network, such as a firewall or server, instead of at the entry point to the network.

Eventually, this situation creates a mess of overlapping authentication systems that are redundant in some places or applications, and might not provide enough identity verification in others. Unfortunately, many network appliances, even those from the same vendor, are disconnected from the authentication infrastructure and don't all work together seamlessly.

The result, for many enterprises, is that guest access is carefully controlled on wireless networks. However, if guests find an Ethernet port in the wall, they have full, unrestricted access. This is certainly not what could be a called a "tight" security policy.

A Flexible Identity Fabric

Although it is vital for organizations to determine which users are accessing what and from where, and to create and manage users' security profiles, doing so is a complex process that consumes a great deal of time and resources. Authenticating application by application after they're already on the corporate network is frustrating to users and expensive to maintain and synchronize. Authenticating on every network box is highly impractical. Even the protocols in wide use today for identity authentication aren't always designed to be very usable and are often difficult to manage.

What is needed are ways to make security profiles, identity, and authentication more coherent and easier to manage. Instead of adding more authentication-specific network boxes to the mix, a better solution would be an extensible identity platform that acts as an "identity fabric"—something that covers all areas of the network that require identity management and wraps around the endpoints but is flexible and scalable, so it can adjust to new devices and protocols.

"Imagine a world where every network box you try to access requires one more layer of authentication," says Calhoun. "That really doesn't scale. From an operations complexity standpoint, people aren't doing authentication on their wired network, so they can't imagine doing it everywhere on the network. So, Cisco started thinking about some sort of 'identity fabric.'"

According to Calhoun, "As the user authenticates at the edges of the network, that information is propagated through the network, so firewalls and intrusion prevention systems no longer have to look at IP addresses or some anonymous thing. Instead, they can attach an identity to it and apply a policy based on who is behind that identity. We're not quite at that point yet, but that's the vision."

This identity fabric or platform will incorporate best-of-breed authentication applications, standards, protocols, and usability options; verify identity at the entry point to the network no matter what device is used (making it future-proof); and seamlessly hand the identity profiles off throughout the network.

To increase the usability, this platform should also offer administrators a more centralized way to manage identity and access policies.

Says Cisco's Stewart, "For identity management to really work, it needs to be simpler to use and deploy than it used to be. And you need good auditing functions, too, so it's easy to know who accessed what when. In these areas, the technology is now becoming easier to use and better, catching up with what we all know we should be doing."

Endnote

[1] "Vint Cerf: the Internet is not secure, 'we don't authenticate very well,'" posted by Jeremy Lipschultz, professor and director, UNO School of Communications, on Twitpic, June 15, 2009. http://www.twitpic.com/7howz.

References

Cisco 2008 Annual Security Report. http://www.cisco.com/en/US/prod/collateral/vpndevc/securityreview12-2.pdf.

Cisco 2009 Annual Security Report. http://cisco.com/en/US/prod/collateral/vpndevc/cisco_2009_asr.pdf.

Cisco Identity-Based Networking Services At-a-Glance. http://www.cisco.com/en/US/products/ps6638/product_at_a_glance_list.html.

Innovations in Cisco Identity-Based Networking Services. http://www.cisco.com/en/US/solutions/collateral/ns340/ns394/ns171/Cisco-IBNS-Overview.pdf.

Chapter 15

Security for the Borderless Network: Making Web 2.0 and 3.0 Safe for Business

This chapter includes the following topics:

- Security Policies for the New Open Networked World

- The Borderless Network Security Architecture

- Super-Charged Scanners

- Security Everywhere in the Network

- Collaboration with Confidence

Now is not the time to *plan* for a mobile Web 2.0 world. It's already here, like it or not. Internet-based collaborative work tools. iPhones, BlackBerrys, and growing numbers of other "smart" mobile wireless devices with multimedia and PC-like capabilities. Social networking, instant messaging, and Skype. Virtualization, cloud computing, and SaaS. Cisco WebEx and TelePresence. Remote and mobile working. These trends, technologies, and tools enable people to work far more efficiently, and be more connected to information and one another, than ever before.

The case studies and the comments from individuals featured in this book reveal that many organizations are proactively trying to find their place in the Web 2.0 world. They are truly eager to leverage new tools and technologies that can increase their competitive edge. They realize the potential these tools have to enable them to streamline their work processes, keep their workforce motivated and productive, connect with their customers, generate significant cost savings, and remain relevant in today's fast-changing global business landscape.

But we have also come to understand that two things are standing in the way of today's workers achieving even greater heights of productivity and creating tremendous value for the enterprise: management's fear and IT's inflexibility.

Many organizations—including those considered leaders in their industries—have been slow to embrace mobile and remote working and Web 2.0, or accept the inevitability of consumerized IT. Some have rejected these powerful forces of change outright, clinging to outdated, irrelevant, and often irrational policies that do little to enhance security. Their policies also make their employees unhappy. And that discontent among the rank and file, more so than any threat that may arise from unauthorized use of Facebook or an iPhone, could turn out to be the most damaging to an organization's success and survival.

Security Policies for the New Open Networked World

As previously discussed, the evolution of technology demonstrates that when people find a tool or process they like or that makes their life easier, keeps them connected to what and whom are most important to them, and gives them a feeling of greater autonomy and empowerment, there is simply no going back to "the way it was before." Today's workers also reject the idea that their "personal" and "professional" use of technology should not be allowed to intersect, especially because they already do—and have for some time.

The irony here is that companies are aware their current security policies are weak. They know their employees are either willingly or accidentally bending or breaking the rules to access whatever they need to do their jobs better. These violations range from the use of unauthorized web-based applications to misuse of corporate computers. Meanwhile, employers also seem resigned that there is little if anything they can do to prevent or control this behavior.

Today's organizations need a new set of tools to express and enforce a more intelligent and relevant security policy that deals with the realities of Web 2.0, social networking, and the anywhere-anytime-any device nature of the borderless enterprise. Without these tools, policies are as effective as the ugly mattress tags that warn: "Do not remove under penalty of law." Most are removed.

At the same time, security that gets in the way of the end user will rarely be successful. Consider this classic picture: A gate is placed across a road with flat, grassy shoulders. Either side of the gate has been worn down by the tire tracks of countless vehicles that have driven *around* the barrier. That's exactly how many users view security measures. They are incredibly resourceful at finding ways to bypass such restrictions in the name of getting their jobs done or living their lives more efficiently. (Consider the admission of a chief information officer of a 60,000-person tech company in Silicon Valley, who reports the organization has 50 "official" iPhone users but 5000 to 6000 "unofficial" users who have found "backdoor ways" to connect into the corporate infrastructure.)

The most effective security solutions can actually *enhance* the end-user experience; if they can do that, users will be inclined to adopt them. To achieve this, modern security systems need sufficient intelligence and granularity, so they can enforce policies that are much more user-oriented—for example, not bluntly blocking access to social networking sites such as Facebook or MySpace, but instead, putting controls on the type of content that can be uploaded from these sites.

As we have clearly seen through the case studies presented in this book, companies create material gains of *productivity* and *efficiency* due to greater workforce mobility and the use of cloud computing and collaborative Web 2.0 tools and technologies.

Increasingly, business is conducted without borders. Thus, the security community needs to adapt and evolve policies so that businesses can embrace these new technologies while not exposing themselves to harm through increased malware infection, acceptable use problems, or data loss.

The Borderless Network Security Architecture

We have determined that security policy needs to evolve to the point where businesses can collaborate with confidence. However, before these more intelligent policies can be developed and fully embraced, the tools to enforce them must also undergo a significant evolution.

As discussed in the previous chapter, next-generation, network-based security systems need to *understand* content, applications, and end-user identity, not just the lower-level constructs of IP address, network port, or network protocol. Cisco has a vision for the next-generation security architecture that will secure the borderless network. These tools are identity-, application-, and content-aware. Simply put, they can tell the difference between CNN and Skype and Oracle. They recognize users and directory structures: John Smith is in sales and can access sales data in a cloud-based application. Joe Smith is in engineering and can access source code on an internal server.

This architecture is comprised of five major components:

- **Scanning engines:** These are the foundation of security enforcement and can be viewed as the workhorses of policy enforcement. They are the proxies or network-level devices that examine content, identify applications, and authenticate users. A scanning engine can be a firewall/IPS, a proxy, or an interesting fusion of the two. Scanning engines can run multiple layers of antimalware signatures, behavioral analyses, and content inspection engines.

- **Delivery mechanisms:** These are the mechanisms by which scanning elements are introduced into the network. This includes the traditional network appliance, a module in a switch or a router, or an image in a Cisco security cloud.

- **Security intelligence operations (SIO):** We're talking now about the "brains" that can identify good guys from bad. The Cisco SIO (described in detail later in this chapter) encompasses multi-terabyte traffic monitoring databases, thousands of servers in multiple data centers, and hundreds of engineers and technicians with a single purpose—identifying and stopping malicious traffic.

- **Policy management consoles:** These consoles are separate from the scanners that enforce policy. By separating policy creation and management from enforcement, we make it possible to have a single point of policy definition that spans multiple different enforcement points such as email, instant messaging, and the Web.

- **The next-generation endpoint:** This is the critical piece that ties everything together. The role of the next-generation endpoint is to reside on a wide variety of devices and make sure all connections coming on or off a device are routed through one of the network-based scanning elements previously described.

Big and Little: The Evolution of Endpoint Security   Traditional network security consists of two major components: a heavy endpoint protection suite (antivirus, personal firewall, and so on) and perimeter-based, network-scanning devices (firewalls, web proxies, and email gateways). This architecture worked well in a world of high-powered PCs that were mainly on the LAN and behind the firewall. But in the Web 2.0 world, enterprise computing devices are changing rapidly.

As discussed in previous chapters, iPhones, BlackBerrys, netbooks, and thousands of other devices are becoming powerful substitutes or complements to the traditional PC. In these highly distributed or lightweight, portable, heterogeneous computing platforms, the traditional "antivirus" endpoint suite is no longer relevant. (In short, we don't want a traditional AV client running on our phones.)

The Cisco security architecture for the borderless network relies on a lightweight, pervasive endpoint. Its role is not to scan content or run signatures. Instead, its sole focus is making sure every connection coming on or off the endpoint is pointed at a network scanning element somewhere in a Cisco security cloud.

These scanning elements are now capable of running many more layers of scanning than a single endpoint possibly could: five layers of malware signatures, data loss prevention and acceptable use policies, content scanning, and more.

The endpoint of tomorrow won't be an antivirus suite, but an intelligent connection manager that sits on the edge of every device imaginable. It is the new perimeter of the de-perimeterized network.

Super-Charged Scanners

The impact that multicore processors are having on modern security cannot be underestimated.

With well-written software, network security applications scale linearly on multicore systems. For example, the throughput obtained from the current generation of Cisco IronPort web security appliances with eight cores is 800 percent faster than the throughput from a single core system just a few years ago.

Multicore-powered systems can now run three layers of antivirus scanning, advanced acceptable use filtering, DLP algorithms, and reputation filtering for 10,000 users on a single two-rack unit appliance. All this processing is done with just eight cores. The security delivered in the network far exceeds what a traditional endpoint can offer: Imagine running three separate AV engines on your PC. It would cause significant disruption to the end-user experience, yet it can be done invisibly in the network.

And there appears to be no limit in immediate sight. The next revision of hardware will support 32 cores, which will be 3200 percent faster than a single core system. This massive surge in throughput far surpasses the needs of traffic increases and makes possible an entirely new class of security scanning that can provide far more sophisticated content analysis. These scanners can distinguish between different types of traffic. They will be able to peer into an application such as webmail and understand the text in the message bodies—looking for information such as credit card or Social Security numbers—with no added latency.

Super-charged scanning elements are at the heart of the new, more intelligent policies required to embrace Web 2.0 and the borderless network safely. They can identify users and their roles in the organization and make decisions on a high level by understanding applications and content. They can enforce a policy that says, "Allow YouTube video streaming for marketing, but make sure it doesn't interfere with WebEx sessions."

Intelligent progressive policies give end users the opportunity to harness the power of Web 2.0, but with logical safeguards. Multicore processors running in the next generation of firewalls and web gateways are the scanning engines making these policies feasible. As these scanners evolve, the distinction between networking devices such as firewalls and web proxies will melt away. They are all simply scanners that reside in multiple points in the network.

Security Everywhere in the Network

Apple's iPhone and Cisco TelePresence are examples of the sexy new technologies that are significantly changing the way we work and communicate. They are also transforming how the network is architected, leading to decentralized Internet access. The traditional architecture of the hub-and-spoke network with a small number of access points is giving way to the borderless network with a large number of access points. As such, modern security needs to be widely distributed across the network.

The Cisco security architecture for the borderless network relies on a spectrum of delivery mechanisms that make it possible to put security in more and more places to accommodate the decentralized, borderless network. The intelligent scanning elements previously described will run as software in a virtualized data center infrastructure. A form factor will be a traditional hardware appliance, such as those commonly used today, and a module in a Cisco networking device, such as a branch office router or a powerful data center switch. Or it will be available as an image in the steadily growing Cisco security cloud, powered either directly by Cisco or one of the many Cisco service provider partners.

Regardless of the delivery mechanism, the scanning capabilities, policy enforcement and management, and the reporting system will be consistent. A customer might choose to put appliances in its headquarters, integrated security modules for its branch office routers, and hosted cloud images for mobile users. These flexible delivery options coupled with higher-level application- and identity-aware scanners enable policy enforcement to be abstracted from the physical network. Users will get the same policy enforcement regardless of whether they are on an iPhone in India or a desktop in Denver.

Security Intelligence Designed In

As discussed in Chapter 10, "Signs of Hope," the next generation of security intelligence requires a broader look at traffic patterns. Using techniques like Cisco's Global Threat Correlation, the ever-sophisticated waves of attacks can be stopped based on the nature of the attacker, not just the nature of the attack. The foundation of this approach is having security telemetry—statistical data about the behavior of the network—built in to all scanning elements in a bidirectional exchange. Traffic data is sent into the Cisco SIO and new rules are pushed out, almost in real time.

The Cisco SIO is a collection of data, machines, and people that work together to identify and stop malicious traffic on the Internet. Now in its tenth year of operation, Cisco SIO is the largest traffic monitoring network in the world. It processes more than 5 billion web requests and 100 million email messages daily, sampling more than 35 percent of the world's email traffic. It has more than 500 engineers, technicians, and researchers working in five facilities around the world. It uses more than 1000 servers and stores more than 2 terabytes of data. This sophisticated infrastructure generates more than 875,000 rules per day. That's about 10 new rules every second of every day.

The scale of this system is remarkable—and it is growing. As Cisco adds telemetry into more networking devices such as firewalls and IPS systems, followed by switches and routers, the sample of Internet traffic will continue to expand rapidly. For every packet that traverses the Internet, there's a good chance it will hit a piece of Cisco equipment somewhere along the way.

This huge footprint gives Cisco unique insight into global Internet traffic patterns. The Cisco SIO is collecting traffic data about every publicly routable IP address on the Internet. Even if all the SIO has to say about a server is "you are new; we have never seen you before," that is still useful information. What it means is don't block the server, but apply maximum content and signature inspection, and feed the results back into the SIO database. If the server is passing legitimate traffic, its reputation steadily climbs. If it is found to be passing malware, its reputation drops.

Cisco's Global Threat Correlation, meanwhile, is the technique of analyzing reputation across multiple realms—email, web, IM, FTP, and so on. The simplicity and robustness of reputation analysis and Global Threat Correlation have enabled these techniques to stop malware, on average, 12 hours ahead of signature availability, and to boost the catch rate of a Cisco IPS system by more than 300 percent. These sustained advances are a result of the broad context that reputation provides.

If a security scanner is attempting to analyze a traffic flow, it is difficult to analyze the bits going by and make an accurate determination based solely on the data traveling past. However, if the system can "look" at where the bits are coming from and going to, make assessments of the client and the server, and identify the application and the content being transmitted, a more accurate decision can be made. This is similar to the manner humans use to analyze threats. When looking narrowly at a brown paper-wrapped package, it can be difficult to know if it is good or bad. But looking at where it is being sent, where it is from, who is delivering it, and what's inside of it provides a much more complete picture. The Cisco SIO provides a comprehensive view of the Internet-facing side of any transaction.

In the borderless network security architecture, all Cisco security devices will have this contextual capability built in. This means every device will know more about who is sending and who is receiving the traffic, what application it is, and what the content is. With this broad contextual information, the scanners can make far more accurate decisions, stopping even the stealthiest threats.

It also means that all Cisco security devices will be tethered to the SIO. Participation in this network will always be opt-in and default off. But after nearly a decade of operations, experience has shown that the participation rate will be extremely high, keeping the global defense systems of the Cisco SIO pulsing with new data feeds and more accurate rule generation.

The Line Between Policy and Enforcement

Today, most policies are developed around a corporate directory. Marketing can have one set of privileges, engineering another. Individuals can have policy exceptions tied to their presence in a directory server. Directories are a foundational capability in any security policy, yet they tend to be static and lack context. Directories answer the fundamental question of *Who are you?*

As we move to a borderless business, we need security policies that will have a broader context. We want to know not just who you are, but also where are you coming from, when you are attempting to access something, what device you are doing it from, and how you are attempting to access a particular piece of information. Therefore, we need to transition from the "who" of a static directory to the "who, what, where, when, and how" of a borderless network security system.

If each scanning element in the network needs to assess the broad context of who, what, when, and how, collecting and coordinating this information becomes unwieldy. It makes more sense to create a new policy server that stores these dynamic attributes and makes them available to a variety of different devices—firewalls, web proxies, endpoints, and NAC servers. Then, each of these devices can make a more robust contextual enforcement decision from a centralized, dynamically updated set of data.

This architecture has another advantage: It allows an IT team to create policies that span multiple different enforcement points. Thus, a policy can be created around access control that would be available to both a firewall and a web proxy. Or a policy can be created around credit card numbers that would span email, web, and IM. Today, this exchange of policy happens manually. In the borderless network security architecture, the policies flow from the centralized policy store through the operations console of the individual devices.

The Cisco vision is to make the interface between policy and enforcement systems open and built on industry standards. Therefore, if a customer chooses to use a Cisco application entitlement system and an enterprise DLP policy manager from RSA, for example, both should work smoothly with existing network infrastructure.

This is not a small undertaking, however, and it will take years to fully develop. However, centralized policy management and coordinated, dynamic policy enforcement provide the flexibility needed when deploying intelligent policies in the borderless enterprise.

Redefining the Endpoint

A critical component of the secure, borderless network is the security system on the endpoint. As we move to a world in which mobile devices take up a larger percentage of our enterprise computing time, the traditional antivirus client suite on the endpoint doesn't go away, but it does become less relevant.

Again, the role of the next-generation endpoint is not to scan content or run signatures. It simply manages connections and makes sure all content coming on or off a device is connected to one of the scanning elements deployed in one of the form factors and running the policies of the system previously described. The client ties the whole security system together.

The next-generation connection manager takes care of all network connections, enhancing the end-user experience. From an end user's perspective, he or she is always on the LAN—it all "just works." When a user is behind the firewall, the connection manager senses this and does not attempt to create a VPN tunnel or connection. Instead, it takes care of basic network functions such as the 802.1x authentication required to make wireless and wired Ethernet switches work smoothly. It also handles posture checking to make sure the client has up-to-date patches and AV signatures.

When a user closes her laptop at work, and then goes home and opens it back up, the connection manager "wakes up" and realizes it is no longer behind the firewall. It then automatically finds the nearest network attach point. Web traffic gets pointed to the nearest web proxies, application traffic is tunneled via IPSec or SSL VPN into the nearest remote access concentrator, and voice and video traffic are pointed at the Session Initiation Protocol (SIP) gateways.

These attach points can be any of the form factors previously described: an appliance at corporate headquarters, a module in a branch office router, or an image in the worldwide Cisco security cloud. All this is invisible to the end users; they know only that it works and it's easier than before. No more fumbling with passwords and authenticating repeatedly. No more struggling to establish a VPN connection.

From the perspective of end users, they feel that they are always on the LAN. From IT's perspective, they now have control and policy enforcement no matter where an end user might go—on a PC behind the firewall or on a smartphone in Timbuktu. The borderless network security architecture offers consistent policy enforcement, reporting, and inspection. This is a perfect example of improving security while also improving the end-user experience.

The connection manager, working with the other components of the borderless network architecture, yields a next-generation security architecture that enables advanced high-level policy enforcement across the network, independent of the physical infrastructure underneath. It understands users, applications, and content. It has the robustness to make security decisions in the broadest context, looking at the who, what, where, when, and how of a transaction. It has policy that is managed separately from devices. And it has an endpoint solution that works on every major enterprise computing platform—Windows, Macs, handhelds, and tablets. It is a complete solution for the borderless enterprise.

Collaboration with Confidence

Although we have yet to experience Web 2.0's full potential, or to know exactly what working and living in a Web 3.0 world will be like, economists, historians, and industry leaders all agree that handheld computing and advanced collaboration technologies will drive another decade or more of productivity enhancements.

In a recent report, global financial services firm Morgan Stanley concluded that the rise of the mobile Internet is likely the fastest adoption of a new technology in history.[1] Two years after its launch, the mobile Internet has eight times the adoption rate that AOL's dial-up Internet service had two years after its launch. This massive adoption is having a profound impact on the way we work and share information, and how our networks will be designed moving forward.

At the same time, new forms of collaboration such as Cisco TelePresence are forcing companies to rethink how they design networks and where they define the "perimeter." And the highly compelling economics of cloud computing mean more of our data and applications are now—or will soon be—on the move.

All these important trends are driving what will be a substantial change in the way that security policies are expressed and enforced in the future. And the underlying technology that powers advanced security—including multicore processors and Global Threat Correlation—is having a massive impact on our ability to create and enforce more intelligent, robust policies.

The driving force for all this change? The relentless corporate need for competitiveness. Companies are finding significant advantages from embracing mobility and Web 2.0 technologies. But the security policies and the technologies underneath it all need to evolve to keep pace with change, so companies can take advantage of these new capabilities while still maintaining basic controls.

The security architecture for the borderless network is what will finally enable businesses large and small to open their networks, transcend traditional borders, and collaborate with confidence.

Endnote

[1] "The Mobile Internet Report," Morgan Stanley, December 15, 2009. http://www.scribd.com/doc/24129386/The-Mobile-Internet-Report.

Reference

Cisco 2009 Annual Security Report. http://cisco.com/en/US/prod/collateral/vpndevc/cisco_2009_asr.pdf.

Index

C

Q - R

S

T

U - V

W

GO FURTHER, FASTER.
BECOME CERTIFIED.

Stop thinking about your potential.
Realize it. Take your training, skills
and knowledge to the next level. Get
Cisco Certified through Pearson VUE.

Take your Cisco Career Certification exam at
one of more than 4,400 conveniently located
Pearson VUE® Authorized Test Centers
worldwide to experience a no-hassle test
experience. To register at a test center near
you, simply visit PearsonVUE.com/Cisco.

PEARSON
VUE

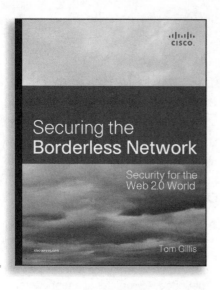

FREE Online Edition

Your purchase of **Securing the Borderless Network** includes access to a free online edition for 45 days through the Safari Books Online subscription service. Nearly every Cisco Press book is available online through Safari Books Online, along with more than 5,000 other technical books and videos from publishers such as Addison-Wesley Professional, Exam Cram, IBM Press, O'Reilly, Prentice Hall, Que, and Sams.

SAFARI BOOKS ONLINE allows you to search for a specific answer, cut and paste code, download chapters, and stay current with emerging technologies.

Activate your FREE Online Edition at www.informit.com/safarifree

> **STEP 1:** Enter the coupon code: QVFOJFH.

> **STEP 2:** New Safari users, complete the brief registration form.
> Safari subscribers, just log in.

If you have difficulty registering on Safari or accessing the online edition, please e-mail customer-service@safaribooksonline.com